Beirut

Jessica Lee

Credits

Footprint credits

Editor: Stephanie Rebello
Production and layout: Patrick Dawson
Maps: Kevin Feeney

Publisher: Patrick Dawson
Managing Editor: Felicity Laughton
Advertising: Elizabeth Taylor
Sales and marketing: Kirsty Holmes

Photography credits
Front cover: imagebroker.net / SuperStock
Back cover: Edwardkaraa / Dreamstime.com

Printed in Great Britain by 4edge Limited, Hockley, Essex

Every effort has been made to ensure that the facts in this guidebook are accurate. However, travellers should still obtain advice from consulates, airlines, etc about travel and visa requirements before travelling. The authors and publishers cannot accept responsibility for any loss, injury or inconvenience however caused.

Publishing information
Footprint *Focus Beirut*
2nd edition
© Footprint Handbooks Ltd
April 2014

ISBN: 978 1 909268 91 3
CIP DATA: A catalogue record for this book is available from the British Library

® Footprint Handbooks and the Footprint mark are a registered trademark of Footprint Handbooks Ltd

Published by Footprint
6 Riverside Court
Lower Bristol Road
Bath BA2 3DZ, UK
T +44 (0)1225 469141
F +44 (0)1225 469461
footprinttravelguides.com

Distributed in the USA by Globe Pequot Press, Guilford, Connecticut

Contents

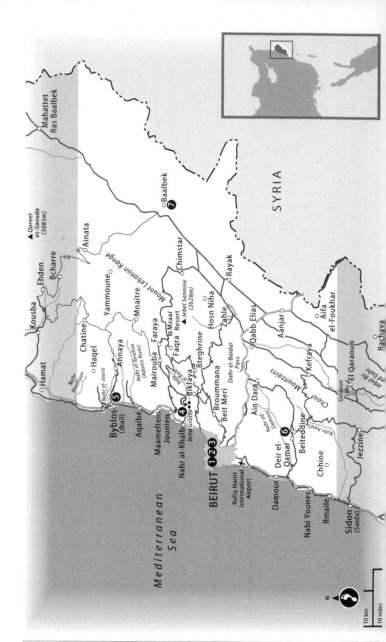

Battered and bruised she may be but Beirut refuses to lie down and play dead. This capital is a chameleon of many faces where trendy bars and glitzy restaurants sit side by side with bullet-ridden and gutted building shells; where the polish and sparkle of the new Downtown district, complete with designer-clad and botoxed shoppers, sits in stark contrast to the Dahiya – the sprawling working-class suburbs which make up the southern section of the city. Beirut, still wearing the scars of war on its sleeve, is the Arab world at its most cosmopolitan and is a proud emblem for Lebanon's remarkable recovery and survival after years of turmoil.

Although much of Beirut's rich history has been obliterated by a succession of natural disasters, invasion and war, there are still vestiges of the past to be found. Peel back the flashy exterior and peeping out from the shadows of the high rises you'll find sedately beautiful and crumbling neo-Ottoman buildings that have, as yet, escaped the developer's demolition ball. The National Museum, although small, is an excellent showcase of Lebanon's antiquities, and among Downtown's pristine streets small pockets of Roman-era ruins, unearthed during the post-civil war development, have been preserved, giving visitors a taste of Beirut's importance throughout the ages.

Lebanon's compact size means that visitors on all but the quickest of trips can discover the country's major sights on daytrips from the capital. The natural splendour of Jeita Grotto's and the ancient Phoenician port of Byblos lie just north of Beirut. While heading inland, through the spectacular scenery of the mighty Lebanon mountain range, brings you to the vast tumbled temples of Baalbek; one of the world's most spectacular Roman ruins.

Planning your trip

Best time to visit Beirut

Beirut's climate is at its most attractive during spring and autumn when temperatures are pleasantly warm and perfect for sightseeing. Heavy rain downpours are common in early spring (March) and late autumn (October) but there are still usually long stretches of dry weather in between. Note that March/April is also the time of the *khamsin*, when hot and dry, sand-laden winds sometimes blow in from the Sahara.

The city gets very hot and humid during the **summer** months of July and August. Summer is also peak tourism season in Beirut; the majority of visitors are regional tourists escaping the even hotter summers of the Arabian Gulf. If you plan to travel at this time, booking your accommodation in advance is advised. **Winters** in Beirut are cool and rainy, with frequent heavy thunderstorms and rough seas offshore. Snow is rare (though not unheard of) but temperatures can regularly drop to below 10°C during the evenings in January and February.

If you're venturing out of Beirut, much of Lebanon's inland regions enjoy an essentially alpine climate. The summer months see the Lebanese decamping to the mountains in droves, exchanging the heat and humidity on the coast for blissfully cool mountain breezes and warm sunny days. The cooling effects of the breezes do not reduce the burning power of the sun, however, and proper protection is essential. Higher up, it gets quite chilly at night, even in July and August. Though temperatures get steadily cooler, the weather generally stays pleasantly dry and sunny right through to November. By December it is cold and the winter rains and snows begin in earnest, usually lasting through to around May, when it begins to warm up again.

Responsible travel in Beirut

Clothing
On the surface, Lebanon seems much more relaxed about dress codes than neighbouring Arab countries, and if you've been travelling through the Middle East for a while the sight of the fashionistas of Beirut dressed in the latest body-hugging and cleavage-enhancing fashions can come as something of a shock.

In the capital and other cosmopolitan areas (such as **Jounieh**, **Byblos** and most of the rest of the northern coastline, much of **Mount Lebanon** and the **Chouf**, and **Zahle**) you can basically dress as you like. If you plan to head out of Beirut to more conservative areas such as the **South** and the **Bekaa Valley**, and the city of Tripoli, it's important to remember that these liberal attitudes do not apply.

The thing to remember when dressing for conservative areas is that shoulders and knees (and everything in between) should be covered. This rule applies to men as well as women. It is also worth noting that the Lebanese place a huge amount of importance on smartness and cleanliness and making the effort to be presentable in public will earn you greater respect wherever you are in the country. See also 'Visiting mosques' below.

Conduct
The Lebanese are generally very open and welcoming and will often go out of their way to help foreigners. Return the gesture by being equally polite and friendly.

Don't miss...

In traditional Muslim culture it is not usual for a man and woman to shake hands when meeting. Instead place your right hand across your heart, which can also be used as a sign of thank you. In traditional areas open displays of affection between couples are not acceptable in public and can cause great offence. Conversely, it is completely normal for friends of the same sex (male and female) to hold hands and link arms in public.

While eating a shared meal, such as meze, it's acceptable to use your left hand to tear bread but the right hand should be used to take from the communal bowls and also to pass things to people. Always tuck your feet in towards you when sitting down. Feet are considered unclean and it's very rude to point them at someone. Also, crossing your legs while seated is considered rude by some more conservative people.

If you're interested in Lebanon's modern history then you're in luck as nearly every Lebanese you will meet is more than happy to talk endlessly about all aspects of local and regional politics. If you find yourself on the receiving end of particularly extreme views, bear in mind that these are people who have lived through some pretty horrific experiences and feelings often run very deep. Note that a great deal of discretion (or better still outright silence) is in order on the subject of visiting Israel.

Visiting mosques Non-Muslims are welcome in most mosques, although in some Shiite mosques they are only allowed into the courtyard and not the prayer hall itself. In any case, always seek permission before entering. Remember that shoes must be removed before entering the prayer hall, although socks can be left on. It is very important that both men and women dress modestly – cover arms and legs (shorts are not acceptable) and, in the case of women, wear a headscarf. At larger, more important mosques, women may be required to hire a full-length black hooded robe at the entrance (and men also if they attempt to enter in shorts).

Getting to Beirut

Air

All international flights into Lebanon arrive at **Rafiq Hariri International Airport**, 9 km south of central Beirut. See page 20.

Flights from the UK Both Lebanon's national airline **Middle East Airlines (MEA)** (www.mea.com.lb) and **British Airways** (www.britishairways.com) have daily direct flights to Beirut. Prices start from around £400 return but can rise during the peak holiday period of June to August, and at Christmas.

Flights from the rest of Europe MEA (www.mea.com.lb) has daily direct flights from **Paris**; **Frankfurt**; **Rome**; and **Larnaca**; and several flights per week from **Athens**; **Brussels**; **Geneva**; and **Milan** throughout the year. During the peak holiday period of May to September they also fly from **Nice** and **Copenhagen**. Return flight prices start from €450 but there is generally a price hike during the June to August summer season. Throughout the year look out for MEA's very good promotional deals which advertise return flights from European destinations for as little as €250.

Other European airlines that fly into Beirut include: from Paris, **Air France** (www.airfrance.fr); from Frankfurt, **Lufthansa** (www.lufthansa.com); from Athens, **Olympic** (www.olympicairlines.com); from Larnaca, **Cyprus Airways** (www.cyprusair.com.cy); and from Rome, **Alitalia** (www.alitalia.it).

Flights from North America There are no direct flights from North America. The cheapest option is to fly into London or Paris and book an onward flight from there. The quickest (though not necessarily the cheapest) option is to book through **MEA** (www.mea.com.lb) who, in conjunction with **several other airlines**, have daily flights from North American cities with a quick stopover in Paris, London or Frankfurt to change planes. Return flights cost from around US$1450. If you shop around you should be able to find a cheaper deal.

There is also the option of flying first into another nearby country and booking an onward flight to Lebanon from there. **Cairo** (Egypt); **Istanbul** (Turkey); **Amman** (Jordan); **Dubai** (UAE); and **Abu Dhabi** (UAE) all have daily direct flights to Beirut with **MEA** and there are often good deals on other local airlines. For example, **Flydubai** (www.flydubai.com) often has flights from Dubai to Beirut for as little as US$150 while from Istanbul **Pegasus Airlines** (www.flypgs.com) offer flights to Beirut starting from US$100.

Flights from Australia and New Zealand Because of the large numbers of Lebanese living in Australia, there are several airlines that fly to Beirut from Sydney and Melbourne, including **Emirates** (www.emirates.com) and **Etihad** (www.etihadairways.com). Return flights start from about AUD$2000. All these flights include a stopover at the airline carrier's national hub.

There are no direct flights from New Zealand; either go first to Australia, or else head for Europe or a city in the region, such as **Amman**, **Cairo** or **Istanbul**.

Transport in Beirut

In Beirut the most efficient means of public transport is by service (shared) taxi. There is also an extensive bus network although some of the routes can be baffling to the uninitiated. See page 22 for further information.

For travels outside of the city, privately operated buses/minibuses ply the major routes between Beirut and all the larger towns. Fares rarely rise above 4000 LBP. The northern Beirut–Tripoli highway and the southern Beirut–Tyre highway are particularly well connected, as is the route up to Baalbek via the Beirut–Damascus highway.

In more rural areas however public transport is extremely infrequent, particularly in the Chouf Mountains region. Unless you've got a bit of patience and some time up your sleeve, hiring a car (or taking a private taxi) is a better option to explore. If you do decide to self-drive be aware that Lebanese driving is erratic at best (and verges on suicidal at times). That being said, if you are a competent and confident driver – provided you are not stupid enough to take on the Lebanese at their own game, it is perfectly possible to drive all over Lebanon (reasonably) safely. See also page 51.

Bus/minibus
Privately operated minibuses/buses ply the major routes between towns with Beirut being the central hub. The only route that has frequent air-conditioned coach-style buses is between Beirut and Tripoli; on all other routes expect a selection of squashy minibuses and beaten-up buses (which often don't have air conditioning).

Car
Hiring a car in Lebanon is comparatively cheap, with rates starting from around US$40 per day for the smallest vehicles. During peak periods (May, August-September and December), it is extremely difficult to lay your hands on the cheapest hire cars; if possible, bookings should be made at least two weeks in advance. Even outside these times, you are advised to book at least a week ahead. On all but the cheapest deals, you can usually get discounts for periods of a week or more.

Conditions vary from company to company. A full driving licence held for at least two years is required by all. Minimum ages vary from 21-25. All require a deposit, either in the form of a credit card imprint, or else cash in the region of US$500. Be sure to check whether the quoted rates include unlimited mileage (this is usually the case for all rentals of three days or more or, in some cases, one week or more).

Insurance arrangements in Lebanon are, In general, reliable (although policies carry a somewhat alarming clause along the lines of "war, invasion and hold-up are not covered"). However, being involved in an accident (even if it is only a low-speed knock in heavy traffic), or having your car stolen, are infinitely more likely scenarios. In either case, you are liable for an excess of anywhere between US$300 (for minor damage to a small car) and US$2500 (for theft or a total write-off of a luxury car).

Most companies offer CDW (Crash Damage Waiver) as an optional extra (usually between US$5-10 per day depending on the type of car); this reduces (but does not completely remove) the excess payable in the event of an accident. Also worth considering is PAI (Personal Accident Insurance), usually costing an additional US$3 per day. Many of the big international car hire companies in Lebanon automatically include CDW in the cost of their hire. Whatever you do, make sure you read the small print before hiring a car. However carefully you drive, there is always the risk of an accident, but the risk of theft can be greatly reduced by always engaging the steering lock and by making use of supervised parking lots in towns and cities.

Avis (www.avis.com.lb), **Budget** (www.budget-rental.com), and **Hertz** (www.hertz.com) all have offices in Beirut, while **Europcar** is represented by **Lenacar** (www.lenacar.com). The main international rental firms all have very similar prices. **Europcar/Lenacar** offers small cars (such as a Renault Clio) with unlimited mileage from US$40 per day. For the same time period a medium-sized car (Peugeot 206 or similar) is US$50 per day and a larger car (such as a Nissan Sunny) starts from US$55 per day. They also do special deals for weekend hire (from Friday afternoon to Monday morning, small car hire costs US$92).

Hitching On any of the major transport routes, hitching is more or less impossible simply because as soon as you stick your thumb out you will attract the attention of any passing service taxi or minibus driver. However, on quiet roads in remote areas hitching is possible and may be your only form of transport. Remember that hitching in the Western sense (for a free ride) is a foreign concept here. Hitching takes place because there is a limited (or non-existent) public transport system in the area, and you should always offer to pay the driver who picked you up. For women travellers, hitching alone can never be recommended.

Service taxis (shared taxis)
For routes between towns, they used to be a lot more prevalent but over the past few years have slowly been replaced by buses and minibuses. They are still useful for journeys to the south from Beirut.

Where to stay in Beirut

There are numerous top-end hotels in and around Beirut and most of the international chains are represented. The capital has an excellent selection of mid-range options, while outside Beirut more and more guesthouses and B&Bs have opened up. It's worth noting that outside of the peak summer season many of the top-end hotels often offer huge discounts (sometimes as much as 50% off the quoted price), putting them into the mid-range price bracket. Unfortunately, unlike other Middle Eastern cities, Beirut lacks a decent range of budget accommodation. Budget travellers are advised to book beds as far in advance as possible to avoid losing out.

Food and drink in Beirut

Food
Lebanon has a well deserved reputation for the best cooking in the region and it is here that you'll get a true taste of what Arabic cuisine is really about. The fusing of Arabic and Mediterranean influences combined with the Lebanese love of food has ensured that eating is always something of a gourmet experience.

Meat, in the form of lamb or chicken, features fairly prominently in the Arab diet, along with staples such as chickpeas (in the form of falafel or hummus), other vegetables, and, of course, bread (*khubz*). Despite the prominence of meat, **vegetarians** can be sure of a nutritious and reasonably varied diet with hummus, falafel, *baba ganoush* (eggplant dip) and other meze dishes, as well as plentiful fresh salads, *fuul* (Arabic beans), and vegetable stews being commonplace on menus.

Seafood is considered a particular speciality in Lebanon, probably at least partly because it is so scarce; during the civil war many people took to dynamiting the fish out of the sea and stocks are still seriously depleted.

Beirut has a high concentration of restaurants, with everything from cheap snack places and Western-style fast-food joints to sumptuously elegant gourmet establishments, with prices to match. As a rule, sit-down meals at restaurants in Beirut cost the same as in Europe. If you're on a tight budget, the city's many takeaway falafel, kebab, and *mannoushi* (Lebanese pizza) stands are great options to refuel.

Drink
Coffee, in its traditional Arabic form, is more widely drunk than **tea**, although both are popular (the latter usually being brewed from a Lipton's tea bag and served in the Arabic way, black and sweet). Beirut also has a plethora of classy and fashionable cafés where you'll find the very best espresso, cappuccino and every conceivable blend of tea.

   Alcohol is readily available and Lebanon has a small but well-regarded wine industry, with the Bekaa Valley vineyards of Ksara, Kefraya and Chateau Musar producing some excellent wines as well as the powerful spirit *arak* (the much-loved Arab aniseed liqueur). There are plenty of locally brewed and imported beers. Almaaza is a good-quality, light lager brewed locally under licence from Amstel. Hops-aficionados should also look out for the artisanal beers by Lebanese microbrewery 961 Beer. Many bars have draught beers on tap, while a few British-style 'pubs' have draught Guinness.

Essentials A-Z

Accident and emergency
Ambulance: T140. **Fire**: T175. **Police**: T112.
Tourist complaints: T1735. In the event of
an accident an official police/medical report
is required for insurance claims.

Bargaining
Lebanon doesn't have as much scope for
brushing up on your bargaining skills as
other Arab countries, which will come as
a relief to some. Many of the souvenir/
handicraft stores are fixed price in Beirut.

Electricity
220 volts, 50 AC. European 2-pin sockets are
the norm.

Embassies and consulates
For embassies and consulates of Lebanon,
see http://embassy.goabroad.com.

Health
See your GP or travel clinic at least 6 weeks
before departure for general advice on
travel risks and vaccinations. Try phoning
a specialist travel clinic if your own doctor
is unfamiliar with health conditions in
Lebanon. Make sure you have sufficient
medical travel insurance, get a dental
check, know your own blood group and
if you suffer a long-term condition such as
diabetes or epilepsy, obtain a Medic Alert
bracelet/necklace (www.medicalert.co.uk).
If you wear glasses, take a copy of your
prescription.

On the whole, standards of hygiene are
good, and the health risks are generally very
low. As a rule, the worst you can expect is
an upset stomach, though more serious
food poisoning or gastric infections are
not unknown.

The standards of private medical facilities
are high. There are plenty of international-
standard hospitals in Beirut and even the
smaller medical clinics are usually excellent.

Note that good medical insurance is
absolutely vital.

Vaccinations
Vaccinations are not absolutely necessary,
but all the same you are advised to make
sure that you are up to date with your **polio,
diphtheria, tetanus, typhoid, hepatitis A**
and **hepatitis B** shots. You may be asked
for a **yellow fever** certificate if you have
been travelling in a country affected by the
disease immediately before travelling to
Lebanon. Malaria is not a problem.

Health risks
Tap water is best avoided unless boiled or
treated first, so stick to bottled water if you
want to be safe. Ice generally gets delivered
in a pretty unhygienic fashion, so is best
avoided. Raw fruit and vegetables are a
potential hazard unless you have washed or
peeled them yourself. On the other hand,
salads are an integral part of
Middle Eastern cuisine and avoiding
eating them in some form or other is
not entirely practical.

Stomach upsets are common. They're
mainly caused by the change in diet
(Middle Eastern food is heavy on oil,
which can be hard to digest for people
unused to this diet). The most common
cause of travellers' **diarrhea** is from eating
contaminated food or drinking tap water.
Diarrhea may be also caused by viruses,
bacteria (such as E-coli), protozoal (such
as giardia), salmonella and cholera. It may
be accompanied by vomiting or by severe
abdominal pain.

The linchpins of treatment for diarrhea are
rest, fluid and salt replacement, antibiotics
such as Ciprofloxacin for the bacterial types
and special diagnostic tests and medical
treatment for the amoeba and giardia
infections. Salmonella infections and cholera,
although rare, can be devastating diseases

and it would be wise to get to a hospital as soon as possible if these were suspected.

In the summer months **heat exhaustion** and **heatstroke** are common health risks. This is prevented by drinking enough fluids throughout the day (your urine will be pale if you are drinking enough). Symptoms of heat exhaustion and heatstroke are similar and include dizziness, tiredness and headache. Use rehydration salts mixed with water to replenish fluids and salts and find somewhere cool and shady to recover.

If you suspect heatstroke rather than heat exhaustion, you need to cool the body down quickly (cold showers are particularly effective) and may require hospital treatment for electrolyte replacement by intravenous drip.

If you get sick
Contact your embassy or consulate for a list of doctors and dentists who speak your language, or at least some English. Good-quality private healthcare is available but is expensive; especially hospitalization. Make sure you have adequate insurance (see below).

Useful websites
www.bgtha.org, British Global Travel Health Association.
www.fco.gov.uk, British Foreign and Commonwealth Office travel site has useful information on each country, people, climate and a list of UK embassies/consulates.
www.fitfortravel.scot.nhs.uk, A-Z of vaccine/health advice for each country.
www.who.int, World Health Organization site with vaccine and health advice.

Insurance
Take out comprehensive insurance before travel, including full medical cover and extra cover for any activities that you may undertake. Keep details of your policy and the insurance company's telephone number with you at all times and get a

police report for any lost or stolen items.

Internet
You'll find internet cafés everywhere in Beirut though some can be noisy affairs with half the terminals given over to kids playing video games. The average cost of 1 hour's internet access is 3000 LBP. Wi-Fi is also extremely common, with many hotels and cafés offering Wi-Fi access for guests, though many will charge for the service. Be aware that the internet service in Beirut, and across Lebanon, tends to be extremely slow.

Language
Arabic is the national language of Lebanon but the great premium placed on education in the country is reflected in the high levels of fluency in both English and French, even in remote, rural areas. Due to its colonial history **French** remains the most widely spoken language after Arabic. However, among the younger generations, **English** is increasingly seen as the more desirable second language.

Money
➔ *€1 = 2086 LBP, £1 = 2504 LBP, US$1 = 1505 LBP (Mar 2014)*
The basic unit of currency is the **Lebanese pound (LBP)**, also referred to as the Lebanese Lira (LL). Notes come in denominations of 1000, 5000, 10,000, 20,000, 50,000 and 100,000. Coins come in denominations of 250 and 500. In addition, the US$ operates as a parallel currency, interchangeable with the LBP, and most transactions (for example in shops, restaurants, bars and hotels) can be made in dollars rather than LBP or in a mixture of the two. Be aware that even if you pay for your transaction in dollars you will usually only get your change back in LBP.

Changing or accessing money is generally very easy, though one exception to this is changing travellers' cheques, which can be difficult.

You'll find lots of banks with ATMs along Rue Hamra and Rue Makdissi in Hamra and there are also lots of money exchange offices in this area. Downtown, you'll find ATMs scattered around the streets leading off Place d'Etoile and banks with ATMs all along Rue Riad es-Solh, while in East Beirut there are banks with ATMs along all the main streets, including Av Charles Malik and Rue Gouraud.

ATMs

You should have no problem finding an ATM in Beirut. Many ATMs allow you to choose to take your money out in either LBP or US$. In general Visa is the most widely accepted card.

Cash

Major currencies (UK£, US$ and €) can be exchanged at banks and at all money changers; the latter will charge you a commission fee, so shop around. The US$ is the most convenient currency and can be used in day-to-day transactions. Notes in smaller denominations are easier to exchange.

It is always useful to have some hard currency with you, for the odd occasion when all the ATMs in town decide not to hand out any cash (rare but not unheard of).

Credit cards

All the major credit cards are recognized. As well as being accepted in most hotels, restaurants and shops, nearly all the larger bank branches in Beirut will allow you to draw money against major credit (or debit) cards and also have ATMs that can be used in the same way.

Currency cards

If you don't want to carry lots of cash, prepaid currency cards allow you to reload money from your bank account, fixed at the day's exchange rate. They look like a credit or debit card and are issued by specialist money changing companies, such as Travelex and Caxton FX, as well as the Post Office. You can top up and check your balance by phone, online and sometimes by text.

Transferring money

Western Union Money Transfer (www.westernunion.com) is represented in Lebanon by Byblos Bank and the Lebanese-Canadian Bank (among others). The fees charged are very high, but this can be a good emergency option.

Travellers' cheques (TCs)

With a plethora of available ATMs, the security advantages of using traveller's cheques (TCs) in Lebanon are far outweighed by the difficulty and costs involved in carrying them. It is a much easier option to use a debit card or currency card as your main form of travel finance and carry a small fund of hard currency as backup.

If you are intending to carry your money in TCs, make sure that you have US$ TCs, as TCs in any other currency are extremely hard to exchange. All banks charge a commission for changing TCs; though the fee is usually only around 1%, they all apply a minimum charge of US$5, and in some cases an additional US$2 'handling' fee. You will also be asked to produce the original purchase slip.

Cost of living and travelling

The cost of living and travelling is more expensive than in other Middle Eastern countries, mostly due to the cost of accommodation and eating. The vast majority of hotels fall into the mid-range and luxury categories (from around US$50 for a double room upwards), with the luxury end of the market being heavily over-represented. That said, there are a limited number of cheaper hotels to be found, as well as a few genuine budget places where you can get a bed in a dormitory for as low as US$20.

Eating out is also comparatively expensive; a meal in a restaurant will generally cost a minimum of US$10 per head, and around US$15 will be closer to the norm, while in the more expensive restaurants, the sky's the limit. To eat cheaply, you have to restrict yourself to a diet of takeaway food and give Beirut's extensive restaurant scene a miss.

Likewise, if you plan to indulge in the city's vibrant nightlife, be prepared to shell out as much for the evening as you would in Europe, North America or Australasia. In contrast, alcohol from a shop (both wine and beer) is actually reasonably priced.

Public transport is cheap, with the furthest journeys costing around 6000 LBP, and most ranging in price from 2000-4000 LBP. Entrance tickets are fairly priced with most sites costing between 5000-12,000 LBP.

Sticking to the very strictest of budgets, it is possible to survive in Beirut on around US$35 per day as long as you use dormitory accommodation, eat only at street vendors and limit your sightseeing. It's more realistic to budget for at least US$50 per day and know that as soon as you start to treat yourself a little, this will quickly rise. A mid-range budget (a/c hotels, restaurant meals and perhaps a hire car) involves a big step up to around US$80 per day. At the luxury end of the scale, you are looking at a minimum of around US$200 per day.

Opening hours

Banks: Mon-Fri 0800-1400 and Sat 0830-1200. **Government offices** and **post offices:** Mon-Sat 0800-1400. **Shops:** Mon-Fri 0900-2000 and Sat 0900-1500, though some will keep shorter or longer hours on Sat and some open on Sun as well. **Major sights:** generally Tue-Sun from 0900-1800 in summer and 0900-1600 in winter, though some sights open 7 days a week.

Prohibitions
Drugs
Possession of narcotics is illegal. Those caught in possession risk a long prison sentence and/or deportation. There is a marked intolerance to drug taking in the country and the drugs scene is distinctly seedy (not to mention paranoid) and is best avoided.

Photography
Avoid taking pictures of military installations or anything that might be construed as 'sensitive', particularly if you are close to the Israeli border.

Safety
Having been emblazoned on everyone's mind as a place of brutal and interminable civil war, suicide bombings and hostage taking, Lebanon is still, years later, trying to shake off its negative media image. Unfortunately, recent sporadic outbreaks of violence caused by overspill from the Syrian civil war and a series of high-profile car-bombings have yet again thrust Lebanon under the media spotlight for all the wrong reasons.

It's important to note that although violent protests and fighting between various factions can, and does, occur intermittently it is usually extremely localised and the large majority of the country, including Beirut, is essentially a perfectly safe place in which to visit. Travellers should keep up to date with the latest government travel advisories before visiting and use good judgement once in the country.

Many foreign office travel advisory sites are currently warning that only essential travel should be undertaken to the south of the country and to certain areas in the Bekaa Valley (including Baalbek) due to several occasions lately when the security situation has rapidly deteriorated with little warning. Before travelling to these areas it is extremely important to keep yourself up to date with recent events on the ground.

Ordinary crime and the threat of personal violence are minimal compared to Europe and North America, though more of a problem than in other Arab countries. Provided you take the usual precautions (never leave valuables unattended in hotel rooms, use hotel safes where available and when hotel safes are not available keep your money and important documents out of sight, on your person, preferably in a money belt or something similar), you should have no problem. Note that petty crime such as bag snatching is on the rise in Beirut, though occurrences are minimal compared to in the West.

If you want to visit one of the Palestinian refugee camps in Beirut, it's best to do so with a well-informed local escort.

If you'd like to visit Lebanon's southern region (outside the scope of this book) be aware that unexploded ordnance is still a problem in the area south of the Litani River, despite a massive demining operation. It is essential that you stick to the roads and avoid walking in open countryside.

Despite Lebanon's reputation, by far the biggest danger tourists face is on the roads. Lebanese driving is erratic at best and absolutely petrifying at the worst.

Tax
Airport departure tax
The airport departure tax of US$42 is levied on all flights from Rafiq Hariri International Airport and is usually included in the cost of your ticket, but be sure to check that this is the case.

Other taxes
There is no land departure tax when leaving from Lebanon.

Most top-end hotels and restaurants charge an extra 10% tax on top of your total, some also add a further service charge.

Telephone
To call Lebanon from overseas dial your international access code, followed by Lebanon's country code 961 and then the area/town code. To call an international phone number from within Lebanon dial 00, followed by the country code.

To call Syria from Lebanon you dial 02 followed by the city code (dropping the initial zero). For example: to call Damascus from Lebanon, dial 0211 followed by the number.

Most travellers are able to use their mobile phones in Lebanon – ask your provider before you travel. Using a phone overseas can be expensive, so don't forget to check your provider's roaming rates.

Lebanon has 2 mobile phone networks: Alfa (www.alfa.com.lb) and MTC Touch (www.touch.com.lb). If you have an unlocked phone you can purchase a local SIM card to use while in Lebanon. Pay-as-you-go SIM cards in Lebanon with both networks cost around US$25 to set up, including credit and 1 month validity, so it's probably not worth doing unless you are going to spend a decent amount of time in the country. Any of the multitude phone shops in Beirut can get you started.

The cheapest way to make local and international calls is by using the extensive network of card-operated public telephones. The cards to use in these phones (Telecartes) can be purchased at most grocery stores. A card with 10,000 LBP phone credit costs 11,000 LBP.

Time
2 hrs ahead of GMT Oct-Mar, and 3 hrs ahead Apr-Sep.

Tipping
Lebanon has a more relaxed attitude to tipping than other Arab countries. In general it is standard to leave a small tip for anyone who helps you (hotel porters, etc) and it's also normal practice to round up your private taxi fare so that the driver

receives a small tip. The standard 10% is acceptable in more expensive restaurants; otherwise it is really down to your own discretion. Remember that the more expensive restaurants often add a service charge onto their bill.

Tourist information
The Lebanon Tourism Board has offices abroad in France and Egypt. They also operate an excellent website (see below) packed full of useful information on Lebanon for travellers. Once in Lebanon, the main tourist information office is located in the centre of West Beirut and is well stocked with pamphlets and maps. There is also a branch at Rafiq Hariri International Airport.

Useful websites
www.destinationlebanon-tourism.gov. lb, the Ministry of Tourism's official website for Lebanon.
www.lebanontourism.org, useful site full of practical information for visitors.
www.lebanontourist.com, informative and helpful site covering the country.
www.tourism-lebanon.com, packed full of information on Lebanon's sights and attractions.
www.fco.gov.uk, homepage of the British Foreign and Commonwealth Office; gives current safety recommendations regarding travel in Lebanon.

Visas and immigration
A passport valid for at least 6 months beyond your intended period of stay is required to enter Lebanon.

Nationals of the following countries are able to obtain a **free single-entry 1-month tourist visa** (which is extendable up to a 3-month period) on arrival at any official point of entry into Lebanon: Andorra, Antigua and Barbuda, Argentina, Armenia, Australia, Austria, Azerbaijan, The Bahamas, Barbados, Belarus, Belgium, Belize, Bhutan, Brazil, Bulgaria, Canada, Chile, China, Czech Republic, Costa Rica, Croatia, Cyprus, Denmark, Dominican Republic, Estonia, Finland, France, Great Britain, Georgia, Germany, Greece, Hong Kong, Hungary, Iceland, Ireland, Italy, Japan, Kazakhstan, Kyrgyzstan, Latvia, Lithuania, Liechtenstein, Luxembourg, Macedonia, Macau, Malaysia, Malta, Mexico, Moldova, Monaco, Montenegro, Netherlands, New Zealand, Norway, Palau, Panama, Peru, Poland, Portugal, Russia, Romania, Saint Kitts and Nevis, Samoa, San Marina, Serbia, Singapore, Slovakia, Slovenia, South Korea, Spain, Sweden, Switzerland, Tajikistan, Turkey (only at the airport), Turkmenistan, USA, Ukraine, Uzbekistan, Venezuela and Yugoslavia. Nationals of all other countries have to apply for a visa before they arrive (50,000 LBP) from the Lebanese Embassy in their home country.

Visa requirements to Lebanon do change sporadically. For up-to-date information see the website of the Lebanese General Security Office, www.general-security. gov.lb.

Note You will not be issued with a visa or allowed entry into Lebanon, even with a visa, if there is any evidence of a visit to Israel in your passport.

Extending your visa
Once in Lebanon, you can extend your 1-month tourist visa. At least a couple of days before your visa expires you need to head to the **Directorate Securite Generale**, on Rue de Damas, across the road from the National Museum. Take your passport, 2 passport photos and 2 photocopies of your passport information page and Lebanese visa page. Visa extensions are handled on the 2nd floor. Come early as it can get very busy by about 1000, and you may have to queue for up to 1 hr. Once processed, you'll be issued with a receipt and told to come and collect your passport in 7 days' time. To collect your passport, bring your receipt with you and, instead of going inside the main building, take the path to the right

of the main entrance that leads around to the back of the building. There is a window here where you queue to hand in your receipt and receive your passport back. You will be issued with a free visa that extends your tourist visa for another 2 months. This is the extension limit on tourism visas. If you want to stay longer you will have to leave the country and come back on a new visa.

Weights and measures
Metric.

Women travellers
Lebanon is arguably the most liberal of all the Middle Eastern countries and on the surface there doesn't seem to be any difference in attitudes to those in Europe or North America. Lebanese women are highly fashionable and the glossy magazine image of the ideal Lebanese woman is one who divides her time between fitness/ body toning activities, hair and beauty treatments, designer shopping and a high-society world of wining and dining. In reality, however, for the majority of the population, the unspoken rules governing relationships and sexual behaviour remain more conservative (among both Christians and Muslims) than initial impressions may lead you to believe. The majority of women live with their families until they are married and most are carefully chaperoned and protected from any possibility of bringing 'dishonour' to the family.

Travelling as a solo foreign woman in Lebanon is in general problem-free and you probably won't encounter any issues. Although you may attract some attention from Lebanese males, on the whole it tends to be good natured and polite. The most common annoyance for solo female travellers is simply the constant questioning of why you aren't married. If you do experience any come-ons that are threatening or unpleasant, make your feelings known clearly and firmly. Like everywhere else in the Middle East this sort of behaviour is considered shameful and not to be tolerated, and you'll find people will run to your aid. Some female travellers have reported experiencing harassment while using public transport, particularly while using service taxis in Beirut. If possible always take the back seat of a service taxi. If at any stage you feel uncomfortable, tell the driver to stop the car and get out.

However liberal attitudes may appear to be towards women's dress in cosmopolitan areas, as soon as you head into more traditional areas attitudes are much more conservative. You will garner much more respect if you wear modest clothing in these areas.

Contents

Footprint features

Beirut

Getting there

Rafiq Hariri International Airport, 10 km to the south of the city centre, is the only airport in Lebanon and handles international flights into and out of the country. There are ATMs, money exchange, at least six car rental firms and a couple of restaurants in the

◻ Beirut: Overview

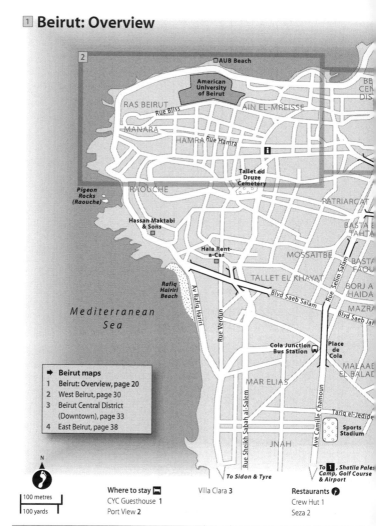

Mediterranean Sea

Pigeon Rocks (Raouche)

Hassan Maktabi & Sons

Hala Rent-a-Car

Rafiq Hariri Beach

RAS BEIRUT
MANARA
HAMRA
RAOUCHE

AUB Beach
American University of Beirut
Rue Bliss
AIN EL-MREISSE
Rue Hamra
Tallet ed Druze Cemetery

PATRIARCAT
BASTA FAHTA
MOSSAITBE
BASTA FAOU
TALLET EL KHAYAT
BORJ HAIDA
Blvd Saeb Salam
MAZRA
Blvd Saeb Ja

Cola Junction Bus Station
Place de Cola
MALAAE EL BALAD
MAR ELIAS
Sports Stadium
JNAH

Av Rafiq Hariri
Rue Verdun
Rue Selim Salem
Rue Sheikh Sabah al-Salem
Ave Camille Chamoun

To Sidon & Tyre

To ◻ , Shatila Pale Camp, Golf Course & Airport
Tariq el-Jedide

➡ **Beirut maps**
1 Beirut: Overview, page 20
2 West Beirut, page 30
3 Beirut Central District (Downtown), page 33
4 East Beirut, page 38

N

100 metres
100 yards

Where to stay ▭
CYC Guesthouse 1
Port View 2

Villa Clara 3

Restaurants ●
Crew Hut 1
Seza 2

arrivals hall. A fast dual carriageway runs between the centre of town and the airport and, depending on traffic, a journey into central Beirut takes around 30 minutes. The easiest way to get into town is by taxi. Official airport taxis (airport logo on the side of the car) and private taxi operators converge just in front of the arrival terminal. The normal fare into the city is US$20 but skilled bargainers should be able to get the price down to US$10-15. At night, or in the early hours of the morning, it is considerably harder to get prices down.

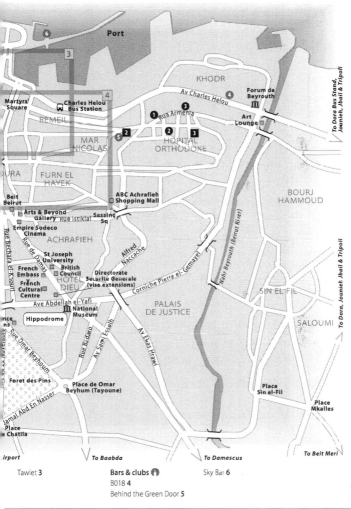

Tawlet **3**

Bars & clubs 🍸
B018 **4**
Behind the Green Door **5**

Sky Bar **6**

To catch a bus from the airport you must walk for just over 1 km to the roundabout at the entrance to the airport complex. From here LCC bus No 5 goes all the way to Ain el-Mreisse (on the Corniche opposite McDonalds) via Cola Junction bus station, Raouche and along the seafront. The journey takes around one hour. However, these buses only run roughly 0630-1730. There are also minibuses and service taxis that run between the same entrance roundabout outside the airport complex and the road junction known as Balbirs (near the Hippodrome), from where there are buses and service taxis into the centre. Again, these only run during the day. ▸▸ *See Transport, page 50.*

Getting around

Beirut isn't the easiest city to get around, to say the least. New arrivals are usually confused by the spaghetti sprawl of different districts and the rocket-pace of the traffic, which makes crossing the road an adventure in itself. Unfortunately the public transport system – provided by a mix of service taxis, public and private buses and microbuses – doesn't help, and even a lot of the locals seem to be stumped by the seemingly mysterious routes of some of the buses. A list of some of the more handy bus routes is given on page 51.

The easiest (and most popular) form of public transport is the spluttering **service taxis**. These shared taxis buzz around the roads of the city constantly picking up passengers. All you do is wait by the side of the road and wave one down. When the driver slows down, shout the name of your destination and he'll either stop for you to get in or speed away. If the first one doesn't want to take you there'll soon be another car trundling along. Make sure you say *'serveece'* to the driver when you get in. Otherwise he may try to take you as a private taxi passenger.

Service taxi trips can be long and circuitous due to route changes based on the passengers picked up. If you want to go directly to your destination, all service taxis can be hired as a private taxi. Obviously as a private passenger you will pay a lot more for your fare. See page 52 for more information on service taxis.

There are also various companies that operate **private taxis** inside the city. These are distinguishable by their colour (usually yellow or white) and the company insignia along the car's body. They usually have air conditioning and are in a much better condition than the older service taxis. You can hail them off the street or you can phone them to book a pickup.

Although it may seem daunting at first, Beirut can actually be a great city for walking. The trick is to catch a taxi or service taxi for the journeys between the districts and then set off on foot to explore. In particular, the districts of Hamra, Ras Beirut and Gemmayze are funky and happening places to wander around.

Orientation

Beirut forms a headland bounded to the north and west by the Mediterranean and to the east by the southernmost reaches of Mount Lebanon. Today the Green Line that divided Beirut (marked by Rue de Damas) is still distinguishable by the concentration of bullet-pocked and bombed-out buildings that lie along it, and while it no longer exists as a physical barrier, the division of the city between Christian east and Muslim west is as marked as ever.

West Beirut is focused on Hamra, which following the destruction of the old Downtown area became the business and commercial centre of the city with most of the hotels, restaurants, banks, shops and other services. To the north of Hamra are the grounds of the American University of Beirut (AUB), while to the west are the exclusive districts of

Ras Beirut and Manara overlooking the western Mediterranean seaboard. Ain el-Mreisse forms a small area to the northeast of Hamra, while extending to the east of it is the new Downtown area, now known as the Beirut Central District. At its eastern edge is Beirut's port complex. Extending south from the port up the hill are the Christian areas of East Beirut, a series of districts climbing up to Achrafieh, the most elegant of them. Sprawling south towards the airport are the poverty-stricken and ramshackle southern suburbs (known collectively as the *dahiya*), home to the city's Shiite population and the Palestine refugee camps.

Tourist information

Tourist information office ① *ground floor of the Ministry of Tourism building, corner of Rue Banque du Liban/Rue de Rome, T01-340940, www.destinationlebanon.gov.lb, summer Mon-Sat 0800-1800, winter 0800-1600*. You have to walk through the ground floor car park to get to the office. They have a good selection of pamphlets on all the main tourist attractions in Lebanon, as well as a decent free map of Beirut. The staff are generally friendly and helpful, although their usefulness in terms of practical information and advice is somewhat limited. The **tourist police** are based in the same building.

Background

Pre and early history Various stone implements discovered in the vicinity of Beirut reveal evidence of human activity dating back as far as the **Palaeolithic** era, although exactly when a permanent settlement was first established here is not known. Excavations in the redevelopment area of central Beirut have revealed traces of a **Canaanite** settlement, the earliest phases of which appear to go back to the 19th-18th century BC.

In the **Phoenician** period after around 1200 BC, despite its favourable location close to reliable water sources and with a sheltered natural harbour, Beirut was largely eclipsed by the more important Phoenician cities of Sidon, Tyre and Byblos. Certainly, the historical record is all but silent as to its fate, while the other coastal cities find frequent mention in Assyrian, Babylonian and Persian records. Although not mentioned in accounts of Alexander the Great's conquest of the coastal cities, Beirut does reappear in later **Hellenistic** records, named *Laodicea in Canaan*, possibly by the Seleucid emperor Antiochus IV in the second century BC (a total of five cities were named *Laodicea* by the Seleucids in honour of a Seleucid queen, *Laodice*). Excavations carried out in 1994 have confirmed that the later Roman city closely followed a typical grid pattern of streets that was essentially of Hellenistic origin.

Roman Period The city only really began to flourish during the **Roman** period, becoming an important commercial port and military base. It was first conquered by the emperor Pompey in 64 BC. Later, the emperor Augustus (r 27 BC to AD 14, formerly Octavian) placed it under the governorship of Vespasianus Agrippa, the husband of his daughter Julia, raising it to the status of a colony and renaming it *Colonia Julia Augusta Felix Berytus* in her honour.

An extensive city was laid out over the earlier Hellenistic foundations, and baths, markets, a theatre and other public buildings erected. The Herodian kings of Judaea (which was at that time in effect a Roman client-state) financed many of these building works in order to gain favour with the Romans. Veterans from the V Macedonica and VIII Gallica legions were given land and settled there, while the local inhabitants received Roman citizenship and were exempted from taxes. From AD 190-200 the Roman emperor

Septimus Severus established a School of Law at Beirut, and from the early third century the city flourished as one of the great centres of Roman jurisprudence. It was here that the substance of the famous Code of Justinian, to which the Western legal system owes its origins, was developed by Papiniam and Ulpian. Beirut was unique in that culturally it was distinctively Roman, with its Law School and community of veterans, in contrast to other cities where Hellenistic cultural influences remained strongest.

Byzantines, catastrophe and Crusader control Beirut continued to flourish during the **Byzantine** period, not least because of the fame of its Law School, becoming the seat of a bishopric by the end of the fourth century. Its reputation as a commercial centre was enhanced meanwhile by the manufacture and trade in silk. However, in AD 551 the city was all but destroyed by earthquakes and associated tidal waves. The Law School was moved to Sidon and although Beirut was subsequently rebuilt, it never regained its former glory. When it fell to the Muslim Arab conquest in AD 635, it was still a relatively insignificant port, and remained so for nearly four centuries of Arab rule.

In 1110 it was captured by Baldwin I after a lengthy siege, and remained in **Crusader** hands until 1187 when it was retaken by Salah ud-Din. Just six years later, however, it was occupied by Amoury, king of Cyprus, so passing back into Crusader hands. In 1291 it was captured by the **Mamluks** and the Crusaders were driven out for the last time. There were a number of attempts to recapture it during the 14th century, but ultimately when Europeans started to settle there during the 15th century, they came as traders rather than conquerors.

Ottomans and oligarchs In 1516 the Mamluks were defeated by Sultan Selim I and Beirut subsequently became part of the **Ottoman Empire**. However, Ottoman rule was never directly applied, local rulers being appointed instead and given a large degree of autonomy provided they faithfully collected and passed on the taxes that were due. Two local rulers were particularly notable for their role in reviving Beirut's commercial reputation. **Emir Fakhr ud-Din II Maan** (1590-1635) was perhaps the most powerful and famous of Lebanon's local rulers during the Ottoman period. During the 18th century Beirut's fortunes fluctuated, favoured for a while by one Emir, only to be neglected by the next. It began to flourish more consistently under **Emir Bashir Shihab II** (1788-1840). However, he also laid the seeds of his own downfall in 1832 by entering into an alliance with **Ibrahim Pasha**, the son of the viceroy of Egypt Mohammad Ali, who had risen against the Ottoman Empire and was threatening to overthrow it. Britain was alarmed at this upset to the balance of power in the region and the threat it posed to her interests. In 1840 a combined Anglo-Austro-Turkish fleet bombarded Beirut. Emir Bashir was captured and sent into exile and direct Ottoman rule was re-established. The opening up of Damascus to European trade from this time fuelled ever greater commercial activity in Beirut, along with an increasing European presence.

In 1860, the massacre of Maronites at the hands of the Druze, first in Lebanon and then in Damascus, prompted direct European military intervention. French troops landed in Beirut and thousands of Maronites fled to the city for protection. These events led to the establishment of 'Mount Lebanon' as a semi-autonomous province, although Beirut itself remained under direct Ottoman control. With its population vastly expanded by the influx of Maronites, and with an ever growing European presence, Beirut's position as the commercial capital of the eastern Mediterranean was further enhanced.

The French Mandate and early years as Lebanon's capital During the **First World War** the British, French and Russian navies blockaded Beirut's port in an attempt to dislodge the Ottoman military forces from Lebanon. This combined with a series of natural disasters, brought famine to the country on a massive scale. In 1916 the leaders of a local revolt against the Ottomans were executed in Beirut, in what afterwards became known as Martyrs' Square. On the 8 October 1918, eight days after the fall of Damascus, the British army entered Beirut with a detachment of French troops. Under the provisions of the secretly negotiated **Sykes-Picot treaty** of 1916, Lebanon (as part of Syria) was placed under **French Mandate** rule in April 1920. Under pressure from the Maronites, the French promptly created the new, enlarged state of 'Grand Liban' (Greater Lebanon), separate from Syria and with Beirut as its capital. The inter-war years were peaceful ones in which Beirut was able to consolidate its position as capital of the new state.

The Second World War and the Arab-Israeli war The **Second World War** saw the return of Allied troops to Beirut, with full independence only being established for the country in 1946. Since independence the fate of Beirut has always been closely linked to, and shaped by, the country's (and indeed the wider region's) complex and tumultuous history.

The **Arab-Israeli war** of 1947-1949 resulted in a massive influx of Palestine refugees, most of who were settled in camps in the southern part of the city and remain there until the present day. When tensions over support for Nasser's pan-Arab vision degenerated into civil war in 1958, some 15,000 US Marines landed in Beirut to restore order. In 1970 the PLO, having been driven out of Jordan, set up their headquarters in Beirut, launching frequent attacks on Israel and establishing themselves as a virtual 'state within a state'.

Civil War When all-out civil war finally erupted in 1975, Beirut was the main focus for the fighting. The city became divided by the infamous **Green Line** between Muslim West and Christian East Beirut. The devastation and suffering was on an unprecedented scale and continued more or less unabated through Syrian occupation, Israeli invasion and the presence of various UN and multinational peace-keeping forces. Worst hit was the Downtown area, which was literally flattened after 15 years of war. Fighting eventually subsided in 1989 and by 1991 the Green Line had been dismantled, finally heralding a lasting peace.

Modern Beirut Beirut's reconstruction after the war was very much the vision of Rafiq Hariri, prime minister of the country for much of the 1990s. His vastly ambitious plan for the city's new Downtown area, and the massive spiralling debt that his construction plans burdened Lebanon with, have been a highly controversial issue in the post-civil war years.

Beirut enjoyed a period of relative stability from the end of the civil war up to 2005, but the city's calm unravelled on **14 February 2005** when a massive bomb blast detonated outside the St George Hotel on the Corniche tearing apart the passing motorcade of ex-prime minister Rafiq Hariri resulting in his death along with 22 others. The days after the bombing saw Beirut's Downtown area submerged under a sea of rival demonstration rallies with Martyrs' Square the focus for the protesters. Out of these massive demonstrations came the birth of the '**Cedar Revolution**', which resulted in the eventual withdrawal of Syrian troops from Lebanon.

During the Israel-Hezbollah **July war** of 2006 Beirut suffered heavy damage from Israeli shelling. Although the central city area was left alone the Israelis targeted much of the city's surrounding infrastructure with the international airport – along with many roads and bridges leading into the capital – being damaged and destroyed. Israel's main

Visiting the camps

There are Palestinian refugee camps on the outskirts of Beirut, Tyre and Tripoli but the easiest ones to visit are Sabra and Shatila in Beirut's southern suburbs.

In Shatila there is no such thing as privacy. The concrete block buildings loom claustrophobically close from the narrow alleys between. There is only sporadic electricity and the residents have no access to running drinking water. There isn't a hint of greenery here; even the school doesn't have a playground. Yet the resilient inhabitants of Shatila have learnt to adapt and survive in this depressing environment.

Although the camps should never be treated as a tourist attraction, those travellers genuinely interested in the plight of the Palestinians will find a warm welcome. Despite what you may hear, Shatila and Sabra are both open and easily accessible, though it makes sense to keep up to date with current events before considering a visit here. Shatila Camp Children and Youth Centre (www.cycshatila.org) is an excellent contact in Shatila and the staff are happy to help foreign visitors inside the camp. It offers opportunities for volunteers to work with the children and it also runs a guesthouse within the camp for visitors.

Travellers should note to dress conservatively before a visit (clothes covering the body down to the ankles and wrists) and to be especially sensitive about taking photos.

targets in the city though were within the sprawling southern suburbs, known collectively as the *Dahiya*. As Hezbollah's urban heartland and home to their headquarters this area suffered major devastation during the month long bombardment. Hundreds of civilians were killed and entire streets were reduced to ruin. Reconstruction in this area (much of it sponsored directly by Hezbollah and by donations from Iran) has, since 2006, been astonishingly fast.

The period from December 2006 to May 2008 saw Downtown Beirut once again become the focus for mass protests. This time it was Hezbollah-led anti-government factions who took over Downtown, and the massive tent-city set up near the Serail caused a 17-month hiatus to normal business taking place in the city's main commercial and financial district. The protest was only dismantled in May 2008 following the election of Michel Sulieman as president of the country and the formation of a national unity government.

Between mid-2008 and early 2011 Beirut enjoyed a relative period of stability. Hopes that this can be sustained long-term have been unfortunately rocked recently amid the collapse of the unity government (in January 2011 and again in March 2013) and wider issues that continue to shake the entire region in the aftermath of the 2011 Arab uprisings.

Lebanon's long border with Syria, and its own chequered history of divided religious and political armed factions has led to conflict linked to the Syrian civil war spilling across the border on several occasions during 2012 and 2013. As well, in September 2013 the UN stated that at least 700,000 Syrian refugees from the war are now residing in Lebanon, equaling one Syrian refugee for every six Lebanese. The country's northern and eastern regions have so far borne the brunt of the fallout from the Syrian crisis but the capital isn't immune. In November 2013 a suicide bomber attacked the Iranian embassy in southern Beirut killing 22 people. In December a car bomb in the downtown area killed seven people including ex-government minister Mohamad Chatah and injured 50. And on 2 January 2014, a car bomb exploded in the Hezbollah-controlled southern suburb of Haret Hreik killing five and injuring 60. With modern Beirut the embodiment of so many of the hopes and aspirations, as well as the frustrations and fears, of modern Lebanon, the city's survival is very much tied to the wider fate of the country as a whole.

National Museum

ⓘ *Rue de Damas, www.beirutnationalmuseum.com; Tue-Sun 0900-1700, 5000 LBP, students 1000 LBP, guided tours 20,000 LBP. An audio visual introduction begins once an hour, on the hour, in a room to the right of the ticket office.*

Opened again to the public in 1999, the National Museum is the jewel in the crown of Beirut's cultural heritage and a powerful symbol of the city's regeneration. It boasts a superb collection of excellently presented artefacts, with everything labelled in English, French and Arabic, while information boards provide brief outlines of each period.

Background

Situated right on the Green Line, separating East and West Beirut, the museum took a pounding during the civil war. Some of the artefacts were removed for safekeeping when hostilities broke out, while the larger ones, such as the stone sarcophagi and mosaics that could not easily be removed, were sealed within thick concrete shells in order to protect them from damage. After the war the museum was the focus of a massive restoration project. Not only did the building itself have to be extensively repaired, but the museum's collection had also suffered severe damage, not least because the basement, where many items were stored, became flooded.

The audio visual hall in the museum's entrance lobby shows a short video giving a quick history of the founding of the museum as well as fascinating footage of the building at the end of the war, revealing the full extent of the devastation.

Visiting the museum

As you enter, you are first confronted by a large **mosaic** depicting Calliope, the muse of philosophy, surrounded by Socrates and the seven wise men all framed within ornate roundels. Dating from the third century AD, this beautiful mosaic was discovered at Baalbek, in the dining room of a Roman villa. In the central area of the hall, arranged around the mosaic, are four large marble **sarcophagi** discovered at Tyre and dating from the second century AD. The delicately carved reliefs adorning their sides depict scenes of drunken banquets and epic battles from the legend of Achilles, and show a quite remarkable degree of artistry in their execution.

In the hall to your right are various artefacts from the Sanctuary of Eshmoun near Sidon, the most striking of which are the statuettes of young children and babies, offered by parents in thanks for the healing of their children. Dating from the fifth century BC, they already show clear Greek influences, even though Alexander the Great did not arrive in the region until a century later.

Further to your right is the recently (2011) restored hall displaying Roman and Byzantine era statuary and mosaics. Of particular interest is the vibrant and intricately detailed Good Shepherd mosaic dating from the 5th or 6th century. Having been sealed upon the wall during the civil war, the mosaic's bottom left hand corner still bears a large hole left by sniper fire.

The hall to the left of the entrance holds various artefacts from the first and second millenniums BC, including the **sarcophagus of Ahiram**, king of Byblos (10th century BC). Though rather clumsily carved in comparison with the Roman sarcophagi from Tyre, its significance is enormous in that it is inscribed with the earliest known example of the Phoenician alphabet, upon which our own Latin one is based. Many of the artefacts here are of Egyptian origin, or else Egyptian-inspired, notably the stele of the Pharaoh Ramses II, complete with a hieroglyphic inscription, found at Tyre. Dominating the small room at the far end of this hall is a carved Colossus from Byblos, also Egyptian in style. Equally striking is the reconstruction of a marble column base in the shape of a pumpkin, and a capital decorated with carved bulls' heads, both from the fifth century BC Sidon.

Tucked away in the corner to the left of the stairs is a fragment of the Virgin Mary fresco unearthed from a 13th-century church in Beirut. In the corner to the right of the stairs is a Roman carved limestone altar from Niha in the Bekaa Valley, with two lions flanking a central god. Beside the stairs themselves are two graceful and beautifully preserved marble statues, the one on the right being Hygeia, goddess of health, while the one on the left is an unidentified Roman woman, clearly of noble blood.

The **first floor** houses all the smaller pieces. Going round in a clockwise direction, you work your way through the prehistoric eras, Bronze Age, Iron Age, Greek, Roman and Byzantine periods to the Arab Muslim era. The quality and beauty of the displays from all these periods is really stunning, but perhaps most breathtaking of all is the vast wealth of Bronze Age pieces from Byblos.

Particularly striking are the hundreds of gilded bronze sticklike figurines with their distinctive Egyptian style peaked hats found in the Temple of the Obelisks. Note also the beautifully fashioned solid gold axes. It is thought these were presented as to Reshef, the Amoritic god of war and destruction and his consort, the goddess Anat in order to secure their blessings for the continued cutting of the cedar forests. The fact that they are solid gold is an indication of how important these trees were to the wealth of Byblos. Similarly, the jewellery and weapons from the tombs of two Amoritic (early second millennium BC) princes of Byblos, Abi Shemou and Ip Shemou Abi show the extremely high levels of skill and craftsmanship which were applied to making such ceremonial offerings.

Around the National Museum

Beirut Hippodrome and Residence des Pins
ⓘ *T01-632 515, www.beiruthorseracing.com, racing takes place every Sun at 1230 during Sep-Jun, and every Sat at 1330 during Jul-Aug.*
At the turn of the century the Ottoman rulers of Lebanon granted a concession for the building of a race track, casino/private club and public gardens in a section of the large pine forest that then still existed to the south of Beirut. However, it was not until after the fall of the Ottomans in the First World War that a member of the prestigious Sursock family established a race track here. During the civil war the hippodrome fell into disuse, but racing started up again soon afterwards.

The **Residence des Pins** ⓘ *closed to visitors*, an impressive Ottoman-period building just to the west of the race track, was originally intended as the casino/private club, but it was leased instead to the French and used as the ambassador's residence. When the lease ran out, the French obtained ownership of it in exchange for other buildings belonging to them. During the civil war it was badly damaged by tank fire, but afterwards was fully restored and serves once again as the ambassador's residence.

Beit Beirut

ⓘ *Corner of Rue de Damas and Ave Independence, due to be opened to the public in 2015.*

A wonderful example of typical neo-Ottoman architecture, the beautiful old Barakat building suffered heavily during the civil war. With its prominent position along the Green Line, this once grand structure became a favoured sniper spot and the distinctive ochre-coloured stones soon became riddled with bullets.

Left to slowly decay for years, the Barakat building is now being restored to serve as a new cultural space for the city. Known as Beit Beirut, the building will include a museum dedicated to the history of the city.

West Beirut

The **Hamra** district emerged as the new financial and commercial centre of Beirut during the civil war and this vibrant neighbourhood is still a hub for visitors with its excellent cafés, restaurants, shops and a good selection of hotels and services. It is not exactly picturesque and there is nothing really to 'see' as such, but it is buzzing with life.

Rue Hamra, running east–west, forms the main thoroughfare. From here you can explore the rough grid pattern of streets surrounding it and shop, dine and snack to your heart's content. Although practically all the buildings in Hamra are modern and rather ugly, here and there you can see the odd few dating from the French Mandate period; isolated reminders of a more elegant past. Heading down towards the **Corniche** along **Rue John Kennedy** and **Rue Omar ed-Daouk** you pass a number of these peeping out incongruously from among the modern tower blocks, including the old French embassy building. On Rue Omar ed-Daouk you can also see the derelict remains of the old **Holiday Inn** building. Opened in 1974 this hotel was for one year the favoured haunt of holidaying jet-setters to the city, symbolizing all that was glamorous about this Mediterranean hot-spot. Due to its prime position along the Green Line, at the outbreak of civil war in 1975 the Holiday Inn was one of the first buildings to be taken over by the militias. Now surrounded by shiny new high-rises and hotels, the bullet-pocked exterior of this empty shell is a stark reminder of the chaos and suffering of the civil war.

American University of Beirut

ⓘ *Rue Bliss, the main entrance is just to the east of the intersection with Rue Jeanne d'Arc.*

The AUB was first established in 1866 and named at that time the Syrian Protestant College. Founded by the American Protestant missionary Daniel Bliss, it was one of several foreign educational establishments that were opened following the advent of direct European involvement in the affairs of Lebanon in 1860. Others included the Beirut Women's College, likewise founded in 1860 and also in West Beirut (it became Beirut University College and is now the Lebanese American University), and the University of St Joseph, founded in 1874 and located in East Beirut (still functioning under the same name). The AUB gained a reputation over the years as perhaps the most prestigious university in the Middle East and today it remains an exclusive, much sought-after (and extremely expensive) place to study. It continued to function throughout the civil war, remaining largely unscathed (notwithstanding the kidnap and murder of various members of its staff and a car bomb in 1991, which destroyed College Hall, the original building of the college founded by Bliss). The extensive grounds here, spreading down the hillside toward the Mediterranean, provide a wonderful oasis of leafy green tranquillity – a world away from the congestion and noise outside.

The **AUB Archaeological Museum** ① *www.aub.edu.lb/museum_archeo/, Mon-Fri 0900-1700 during term time only, free, bring your passport to gain entry*, houses an interesting collection of artefacts which have been gathered from around the wider Middle East region as well as from Lebanon itself. The emphasis is very much on the prehistoric and ancient periods up until Roman and early Byzantine times; stone implements of the Palaeolithic, Mesolithic and Neolithic periods; varied examples of the pottery styles/techniques of Mesopotamia and Egypt during the fifth and fourth millenniums BC; Sumerian administrative tablets from the kingdom of Ur; pottery, jewellery, figurines and fertility goddesses of the second and third millenniums BC from the Euphrates region of North Syria and from Phoenician coastal sites such as Byblos;

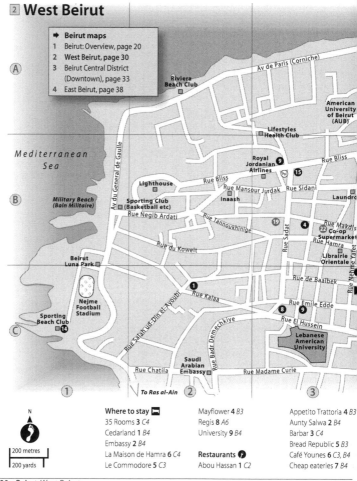

2 West Beirut

➔ **Beirut maps**
1 Beirut: Overview, page 20
2 West Beirut, page 30
3 Beirut Central District (Downtown), page 33
4 East Beirut, page 38

Where to stay 🛏
35 Rooms 3 *C4*
Cedarland 1 *B4*
Embassy 2 *B4*
La Maison de Hamra 6 *C4*
Le Commodore 5 *C3*

Mayflower 4 *B3*
Regis 8 *A6*
University 9 *B4*

Restaurants 🍴
Abou Hassan 1 *C2*

Appetito Trattoria 4 *B3*
Aunty Salwa 2 *B4*
Barbar 3 *C4*
Bread Republic 5 *B3*
Café Younes 6 *C3, B4*
Cheap eateries 7 *B4*

the strikingly more sophisticated later Phoenician fertility goddesses and figurines of the Middle Iron Age (900-600 BC); and Hellenistic, Roman and Byzantine artefacts, including coins reaching up to the Umayyad period. Although many of the artefacts are very impressive, the labelling is unfortunately rather patchy and no attempt has been made at interpretive explanations of the displays.

The Corniche

Running the full length of West Beirut's northern and western seafront, the Corniche is where Beirutis come to exercise, socialize, enjoy the sunset, and generally 'see and be seen'. A stroll here in the evening provides perfect people-watching opportunities.

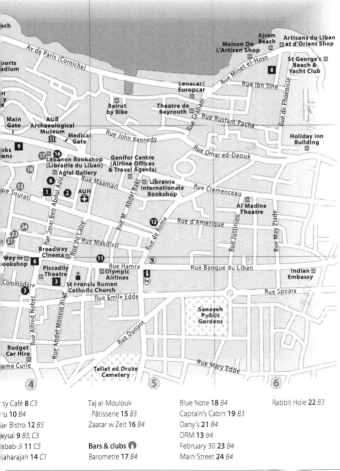

Following it west, the Corniche proper starts from its junction with **Rue Minet el-Hosn** (opposite the Hard Rock Café and McDonald's). The first stretch passes through an area known as **Ain el-Mreisse** after the spring and tiny fishing bay located there (the entrance to the bay passes under the road, so you must cross over to see inside).

Further on is the **AUB 'beach'** (see page 49) and the university grounds stretching up the hill on the opposite side of the road, followed by the flashy Riveria hotel complete with its own private beach club/marina. A little further on the road swings south following the coastline. The small headland here is a particularly popular fishing spot. To the south, the military-only Bain Militaire is followed by a cluster of restaurants, cafés and private beach clubs (see listings, as above), a couple of the latter are just behind the wonderfully retro **Luna Park** fairground, dominated by a large Ferris wheel, and the football stadium.

The road then climbs steeply up to the cliffs that mark this stretch of the coast, known as Raouche, now an area of residential apartments, cafés, restaurants and brightly lit fast food outlets. Just beyond the cliffs, the famous **Pigeon Rocks** rise from the sea, two tall pillars of rock with arches hollowed through them at their bases by the action of the sea. During summer small boats ply the short trip from the shore to the rocks for you to admire them up close. Continuing south, the road descends, down to a long stretch of sand beach, known as **Rafiq Hariri beach** which is open to the public and has no entrance fee.

Beirut Central District (Downtown)

The city centre was largely destroyed during the civil war. Once a thriving financial and commercial centre of offices, hotels, cafés and markets, the entire heart of Beirut was smashed and devastated by the endless rounds of fighting. After the civil war it became the scene of one of the largest urban redevelopment projects in the world with many of the grand old Ottoman and French Mandate buildings painstakingly restored to their former glory. Some of the area (particularly around Place d'Etoile) has been fully pedestrianized, making it a quiet oasis away from the rest of the city.

Background

The redevelopment of the BCD is all the work of **Solidere** (or Société Libanaise pour le Développement et la Reconstruction du Centre-Ville de Beyrouth), formed in 1994 by the late Lebanese prime minister Rafiq Hariri. The primary objective of this private real estate company was to reconstruct the old downtown area of central Beirut in accordance with a government-approved master plan. The highly ambitious and ongoing scheme involves the redevelopment of 180 ha of land including over 60 ha of landfill reclaimed from the sea.

The single greatest obstacle to initiating a redevelopment project on such a large scale was the complex web of local land/property ownership and tenancy rights that existed within the area. In all, more than 40,000 active property owners were involved, while in one celebrated case it was revealed that 4750 people held ownership or tenancy rights to a single plot of land in the souqs. To get around this problem, all those with property rights of one sort or another were given shares in Solidere, amounting to a total value of US$1.17 billion, this being the estimated total value of private real estate in the BCD. In addition, outside investors were allowed to buy shares in the company to a value of US$650 million.

Solidere is responsible for carrying out all infrastructure works (roads, tunnels, bridges, public squares, gardens, etc), and also for treating the landfill on the reclaimed land and developing the sea defences and two associated marinas. In the historic core of the district (centred on Place d'Etoile), it has restored more than 250 Ottoman and French Mandate period buildings in an effort to preserve as much of the historic core of the city in its original form and layout as possible.

The redevelopment of the whole of the centre of the city presented archaeologists with a unique excavation opportunity. Remains from every period of occupation from the Canaanite period onwards were uncovered, and provisions were included in the master plan to preserve as much as possible of these remains in the form of archaeological gardens within the centre.

However, perhaps inevitably for an undertaking of this size, the project has drawn a great deal of criticism. Former property owners in the project area have claimed that the real value of land and property has been massively underestimated, describing Solidere as having pulled off the "biggest land-grab in history". At the same time, the differing priorities of archaeologists keen to uncover and preserve as much as possible, and developers impatient to get on with the job of rebuilding the city centre, have led at times to tensions and even hostilities.

Smaller concerns include the lack of recreational facilities here, which would bring some life to the area. For the most part, the new BCD consists of high-end shops and office blocks that don't exactly bring the Beruitis thronging to the centre. On the outskirts of the centre the area is still a massive construction zone, with cranes dominating the

③ Beirut Central District (Downtown)

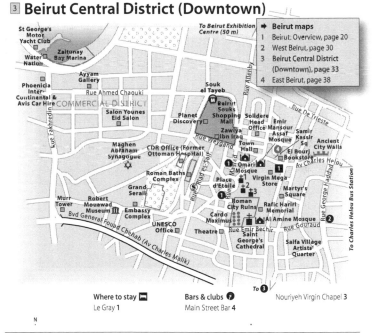

➡ **Beirut maps**
1 Beirut: Overview, page 20
2 West Beirut, page 30
3 Beirut Central District (Downtown), page 33
4 East Beirut, page 38

Where to stay 🛏
Le Gray 1

Bars & clubs 🎵
Main Street Bar 4

Nouriyeh Virgin Chapel 3

skyline, huge billboard fences covering whole blocks and advertising new apartment complexes, and the steady thump of concrete mixers echoing in the air. It is estimated that the entire finished plan won't be completed for another 30 years.

Place d'Etoile

Place d'Etoile and the streets radiating from it have been completely restored. Thought to stand on the site of the forum of the Roman city, this area was laid out in its present form by the French, with the north-south Rue Maarad being modelled on the Rue de Rivoli in Paris. Today, the architecture is striking, combining the quiet grace and elegance of restored Ottoman and French Mandate period buildings with the loud modernity of glass and steel office blocks. All along **Rue Maarad** and the surrounding streets are street-side cafés, fancy restaurants and expensive boutiques, which are just as at home here as they would be in Paris or Rome. This area is completely closed off to traffic, creating a surreally tranquil bubble right in the heart of the city. The best time to visit is during the early evening when Place d'Etoile and the surrounding streets come alive with local families utilizing the car-free streets for strolling and impromptu games of football. At other times the entire area can seem quite dead and soulless.

On the eastern side of the square is **St George Greek Orthodox Cathedral** ① *daily 1000-1800, free, church museum 5000 LBP*. Built on the site of the fifth-century Anastasis Cathedral, St George is Beirut's oldest church. After the civil war it was rebuilt and its early 20th-century interior frescos completely restored. The iconostasis is richly decorated and holds older paintings of saints that were gifted from monasteries in Cyprus and St Katherine's in Egypt's Sinai. Below the church is the **Crypt Museum**. Archaeological work on this site after the civil war unearthed finds from the Hellenistic through to the Ottoman era including mosaic flooring thought to be part of the Anastasis Cathedral, and necropolises dating from the medieval and Mamluk periods. There is also an interesting audio visual presentation which documents the long history of this place of worship and shows the devastation of the cathedral after the war.

Next door to the cathedral is **St Elie Greek Orthodox Church** ① *daily 1000-1800, free*. First built in 1863, the interior is notable for its neo-classical interior and simple yet stunning translucent marble windows. Behind both churches hides the tiny Nuriyeh Chapel, dedicated to the Virgin Mary.

Grand Serail and Roman baths

On an area of higher ground to the west of Place d'Etoile, overlooking the old centre of Beirut, is the **Grand Serail**. This was built in 1890 and acted both as a barracks and the seat of the Ottoman government. Following independence it served as the Ministry of Interior. The building now houses the Council of Ministers and the prime minister's offices and is surrounded by heavy security. The smaller building immediately to the north of it was the Ottoman military hospital and now houses the Council for Development and Reconstruction (CDR), responsible for coordinating these activities at a national level.

Between the Grand Serail and Rue Riad es-Solh there is a long, narrow area of excavations where the remains of a **Roman baths** complex have been uncovered, preserved today as an archaeological 'garden'. The three rooms identified as the *caldarium, tepidarium* and *frigidarium* can be clearly discerned, along with the under-floor *hypocaust* (or heating system) consisting of raised floors supported on miniature pillars of discs. The channels cut into the surrounding bedrock in order to direct the flow of water can also be made out, along with a huge stone basin and traces of mosaics.

Just west of the Grand Serail, among a redeveloped area of presently empty new office blocks and apartment buildings that remains cordoned off to traffic due to its close proximity to the Serail is the **Maghen Abraham Synagogue**. The synagogue has been fully restored (although it isn't open to the public) and is one of the last reminders of Beirut's once vibrant Jewish community.

Robert Mouawad Private Museum
① *Rue Armee, T01-980970, www.rmpm.info, Tue-Sun 0900-1700, 10,000 LBP.*
The passionate collector Henri Pharaon spent a lifetime amassing this eclectic assortment of ceramics, antiques, art and typical Arabic craftwork inside his grand villa known as the Pharaon Palace. After his death, jeweller Robert Mouawad turned the residence into a museum. If you're interested in Arabic interiors this villa is definitely worth a visit. Henri Pharaon spent years transforming his European-style residence into a traditional Arabic mansion, collecting and restoring fine examples of wooden decorative wall panels and hand-painted tile work for the interior.

Waterfront
The rejuvenated marina is the latest part of Solidere's redevelopment of the Downtown area. **Zaitunay Bay**, running along the Corniche just to the east of St Georges Hotel, is a glossy shorefront promenade of restaurants and cafés looking out onto the new marina chock-a-block full of yachts.

Further along the waterfront is **Beirut Exhibition Center** ① *daily 1100-2000, free*. The centre hosts a program of temporary art exhibitions throughout the year. See page 47 for further details.

Beirut Souk (old souqs area)
At its north end, Rue Riad es-Solh intersects with the east-west Rue Weygand. To the north of Rue Weygand is what used to be the old souqs area and is now the exceedingly glamorous Beirut Souks shopping arcade where dressed-to-the-nines Beirutis come to browse the high-end shops and foreign clothing outlets. Every Saturday Beirut Souks plays host to the excellent **Souk El-Tayeb** farmer's market. See page 49 for more details.

Excavations have revealed that a market and complex of artisans' workshops existed here even from pre-Hellenistic times. Traces of Ottoman silk workshops, as well as Mamluk potteries and glass-blowing workshops were found, along with late Roman and Byzantine houses and shops, often with elaborate mosaic floors. Rue Weygand has in fact been shown to follow almost exactly the line of the Roman *decumanus*, while Souq Tawile ('Long Souq') also existed on this alignment from the Hellenistic period.

On the edge of the souqs area, immediately opposite the intersection of Rue Riad es-Solh and Rue Weygand, is the **Zawiye Ibn Iraq**, a small domed sanctuary dating from 1517 and the only Mamluk-period monument to survive in Beirut. Attributed to a Sufi religious authority named Ibn Iraq al-Dimashqi, it is thought to have served as a *zawiye*, or Sufi religious school. Along the west side of the souqs area there are traces of the medieval walls which once surrounded the old city. These have also been preserved in an archaeological 'garden'.

Omari Mosque and around
Heading east along Rue Weygand, on the south side of the road, is the **Omari Mosque** ① *entry on Rue Maarad*. Visitors should be respectfully dressed to enter and women

should cover their hair, gowns are given at the door for anyone wearing shorts or other inappropriate dress. This mosque was originally built in the mid-12th century by the Crusaders as the Church of St John the Baptist (on the site of an earlier Byzantine church which was itself built on the foundations of the Roman temple of Jupiter). In 1291, after the Mamluks had finally driven the Crusaders from Beirut for the last time, it was converted into a mosque. There are clear indications of its earlier use as a Christian place of worship in its cross-shaped plan as well as the many Byzantine architectural features which have been incorporated.

One further block along Rue Weygand is the **Emir Mansour Assaf Mosque**, built in the 16th century by the Ottoman governor Emir Mansour Assaf. Like the Omari Mosque, this mosque first began life as the Byzantine Church of the Holy Saviour and the merging of architectural styles can still be seen in its interior.

Samir Kassir Square

Further east along the same street is a tiny landscaped square dominated by a statue of Samir Kassir; an outspoken journalist who was killed by a car bomb on 2 June 2005. A leading vocal critic of Syrian intervention within Lebanon, Kassir's murder is most often attributed to Syrian or pro-Syrian factions. The movingly simple tribute, which lays just a stone's throw from the An Nahar newspaper building where he once worked, is a fitting constant reminder of the dangers journalists in Lebanon face when daring to expose the truth. Just to the right of the statue are two quotes. Before the death of Rafiq Hariri, Kassir devoted much of his writing to condemning Solidere's redevelopment of Downtown and what he saw as the reckless destruction of the city. The first quote, in French, refers to this, translating as "Beirut, outward in its wealth, the city that is also outward in its ruins." The second, more poignant, quote in Arabic is his rallying cry to the Lebanese, written just after the murder of Hariri: "Return to the streets, dear comrades, and you will return to clarity."

Solidere information centre

ⓘ *In the grid of pedestrian streets to the north of Rue Weygand, Mon-Fri 0900-1800, free.*
The Solidere information centre boasts a huge and elaborate scale model of the BCD, which gives an excellent overview of the area and the controversial and ongoing redevelopment, as well as more detailed scale models of different areas, and even individual buildings.

Cardo Maximus archaeological site

Immediately to the left of St George Maronite Cathedral, as you face it on Rue Emir Beshir, a number of re-erected columns mark the **Cardo Maximus** of the Roman city. This area between Martyrs' Square, the Maronite cathedral and Al Amine Mosque, and St George Greek Orthodox Cathedral was the focus of intensive excavations after the civil war that have uncovered a large portion of the Roman market area and the remains of a number of important buildings.

There are plans to turn this area into a Garden of Forgiveness in memorial to the city's war and where the ruins, amid landscaped gardens, will be properly preserved. So far though, the ruins remain fenced off and are best viewed from either beside St George Maronite Cathedral or from the street running north from beside the Cardo Maximus columns to St George Greek Orthodox Cathedral.

St George's Maronite Cathedral

To the southeast of Place d'Etoile, on Rue Emir Bechir, before you reach Martyrs' Square, is the Maronite Cathedral of St George. Heavily damaged during the war, it has been completely restored to its former glory. In its present form it dates from 1890, though it stands on the site of an older Maronite church built during the early 18th century. The towering façade is modelled on the Santa Maria Maggoria in Rome.

The interior, with its richly decorated ceiling and vast expanses of marble, is both lavish and yet at the same time somehow austere. On the apse wall is a large painting of St George slaying the dragon.

Al Amine Mosque

① Visitors should be respectfully dressed to enter and women should cover their hair, gowns are given at the door for anyone wearing shorts or other inappropriate dress.

Next door to the Maronite cathedral and towering over Martyrs' Square on its western side is the modern Al Amine Mosque; sometimes called the Rafiq Hariri Mosque or the Blue Mosque. It was finished in 2008 and is Lebanon's largest mosque with a vast interior prayer hall that can accommodate 3800 people. The architecture and interior are inspired by classical Ottoman mosque design.

Just to the side of the mosque, under a temporary shelter, is the **memorial tomb** of ex-prime minister Rafiq Hariri himself.

Martyrs' Square and around

Although not much to look at (just a bare area of gravel really), Martyrs' Square is Lebanon's most famous congregation point and was the social focal point of old Beirut. This is where the famous Lebanese singer Fayrouz performed in 1994, in a concert that embodied the re-emerging peace and unity of the city. This is also where an approximate one million Lebanese converged on 14 March 2005 to commemorate the one-month anniversary of Rafiq Hariri's death and protest against Syrian interference in the country.

Popularly known in Arabic as 'Al Bourj' (literally 'tower'), after a medieval watchtower that once stood at its southern end, it was later known as the 'Place des Cannons', when a huge cannon was set up here in 1772 during a brief occupation of the city by the Russian fleet of Catherine the Great. The name Martyrs' Square dates from the execution here of the leaders of the rebellion against Ottoman rule in 1840. A statue commemorating the martyrs stands in the square. During the civil war the square laid right on the Green Line; the statue was riddled with bullet holes but remained standing, becoming a poignant symbol of the city's suffering. It was restored after the war (but the bullet holes have been left intact) and returned to its original place.

Heading east from Martyrs' Square along Avenue Charles Helou, if you look over the north side of the avenue, you can see below you traces of the ancient **Canaanite and Phoenician city walls**. In the corner, by the point where the avenue crosses over Rue George Haddad, are the foundations of a later circular tower.

East Beirut

Rue de Damas marks the boundary between East and West Beirut; the various districts of East Beirut extending south up the hillside from the main port area. Along with Hamra, this is one of the main nightlife areas, with Gemmayze and Monot in particular packed full of restaurants, cafés, bars and clubs. Unlike West Beirut, it has also managed to retain far more of its Ottoman and French Mandate architecture, giving a taste of what the city was like before it was overtaken by developers. The most striking example of the opulent architecture of the late Ottoman period can be seen in the Sursock Museum building and in a number of the other houses along Rue Sursock.

Sursock Museum

ⓘ *Rue Sursock, T01-334133. Closed at time of research; it is due to be opened again in 2014.*
The strikingly elegant building in which this privately run museum is housed is one of several to be found around this affluent quarter of Christian East Beirut, but is of special

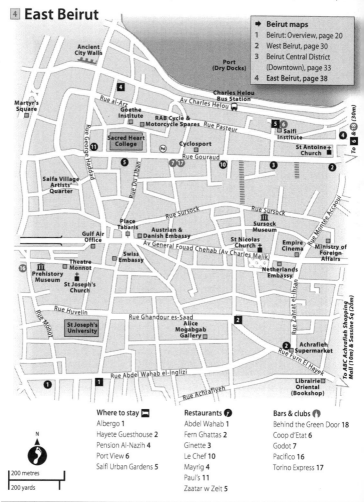

4 East Beirut

→ Beirut maps
1 Beirut: Overview, page 20
2 West Beirut, page 30
3 Beirut Central District (Downtown), page 33
4 East Beirut, page 38

Where to stay 🛏
Albergo **1**
Hayete Guesthouse **2**
Pension Al-Nazih **4**
Port View **6**
Saifi Urban Gardens **5**

Restaurants 🍴
Abdel Wahab **1**
Fern Ghattas **2**
Ginette **3**
Le Chef **10**
Mayrig **4**
Paul's **11**
Zaatar w Zeit **5**

Bars & clubs 🍸
Behind the Green Door **18**
Coop d'Etat **6**
Godot **7**
Pacifico **16**
Torino Express **17**

interest in that it is open to the public. Built in 1902, it was dedicated as a museum on the death of its owner Nicolas Ibrahim Sursock in 1952 and since then has been maintained by the Sursock family as a museum (or, more accurately, a gallery of contemporary art). There is a small permanent exhibition that's supplemented by annual retrospective, foreign and other exhibitions. As well as being worth a visit simply to see the building, the exhibitions give an interesting insight into contemporary Lebanese art.

St Joseph University Prehistory Museum
ⓘ *St Joseph University Street, T01-421860, www.usj.edu.lb/mpl, Tue-Fri 0830-1500; Sat 0830-1300, 5000 LBP, students 3000 LBP.*
This museum – part of the St Joseph University campus – holds an interesting collection of prehistoric artefacts unearthed at archaeological sites across the country. The exhibits trace the history of Neolithic man in the Middle East from hunter-gatherer to the beginning of agriculture.

Outside the central city

Cilicia Museum
ⓘ *Antelias highway, Tue-Sat 0900-1500, Sun 0900-1300, free (bring passport to gain entry), to get here any of the white minibuses travelling up the Antelias highway can be hailed from near the petrol station on the corner of Av Charles Helou and Rue Al Khodr (off Rue Armenia) or LCC No6 bus travels via the Antelias highway on its way to Byblos; get off the bus once you're on the highway at the second road overpass, the Holy See of Cilicia compound is 2 blocks up on the right-hand side of the road (you can see the church steeples from the overpass).*
Since 1930, after the destruction of the Monastery of St Sophia of Sis near present-day Adana in Turkey, this rather mundane location, on the main highway heading north out of Beirut, has been home to the Holy See of Cilicia, the seat of the Armenian Apostolic Church.

Inside the complex (left of the entry) is the beautiful and engrossing Cilicia Museum, which contains an incredible collection of religious artefacts including a horde of old manuscripts and bibles, relics of various saints and some sumptuous gold-embroidered textiles.

The museum is well worth a visit as much for the story behind the artefacts displayed as the items themselves. Although labelling is poor throughout, a guide (compulsory) accompanies you within the museum and explains the history behind the more major exhibits.

Much of what is displayed here was what the monks of the Monastery of St Sophia of Sis could salvage and then smuggle out of Turkey, with great risk, on their long walk overland into Syria.

Beirut listings

For hotel and restaurant price codes and other relevant information, see pages 10-11.

● Where to stay

Beirut *p20, maps p20, p30, p33 and p38*
Accommodation is, in general, expensive and unless yryou're in the top-end bracket of the market don't expect your hotel room to come with all bells and whistles attached. Price ranges for hotels below are based on high-season (Jul-Aug) official full room rates but even in mid-Aug discounts and special offers are sometimes available.

Reserving your room in advance is always worthwhile as all the decent hotels tend to be booked out constantly. It's also worth remembering that outside of high season most of the city's mid-range and some of the top-end hotels drop their prices substantially.

Luxury hotels mostly congregate around Hamra, the BCD (Downtown), along the Corniche and in Achrafieh. Mid-range accommodation is based in Hamra. We've included the best of the city's budget choices, but if you're really down to your last pennies there are more budget hotels around the Port Area just off Av Charles Helou. Most deal mainly in beds for migrant workers but they're used to backpackers wandering in. If you're a single female traveller on a budget it's safer to stick to the options listed below.

Beirut's more expensive hotels all charge a hefty service and government tax on top of the room rate. This has been included in the prices below. All rooms come with attached bathroom as standard unless otherwise stated.

$$$$ Albergo, 137 Rue Abdel Wahab el-Inglizi, Achrafieh, T01-339797, www. albergobeirut.com. Set in a beautifully restored Ottoman-period mansion, the Albergo is a taste of the opulent days gone by but with modern luxuries. Gorgeous lamps, colourful textiles, modern art and antiques all mix and mingle beautifully, giving a totally individual look to each of the high-ceilinged rooms. By far Beirut's most special hotel experience. Restaurant, rooftop terrace with swimming pool and bar, Wi-Fi, parking. Recommended.

$$$$ Le Gray, Martyrs' Sq, Downtown, T01-971111, www.campbellgrayhotels. com. Beirut's hipster hotel is slap in the centre of Downtown. Le Gray oozes classy contemporary chic with its fresh modern interiors warmed up by clever splashes of coloured textiles. As you'd expect, rooms are equipped with all the latest gadgets and technology while bathrooms are fit for a princess with spacious walk-in showers and their own TVs. With commanding views over the surrounding cityscape, the rooftop swimming pool and its swish sun terrace is the perfect retreat from the chaos of the city. Fabulous restaurants, spa, bar, Wi-Fi, parking.

$$$$ Villa Clara, Rue Khenchara, off Rue Armenia, Gemmayze, T70-995739, www. villaclara.fr. This boutique hotel is perfect for those seeking a more intimate Beirut experience. On a quiet side street, the distinctive blue early 20th-century villa is home to 7 high-ceilinged rooms with more than a hint of bohemian-chic. Earthy colours, beautiful artwork and decorative designer pieces all add to the appeal. Breakfast included, Wi-Fi, parking.

$$$ 35 Rooms, Rue Commodore, Hamra, T01-345676, www.35rooms.com. Dominated by a purple interior theme, 35 Rooms (which, unsurprisingly, has 35 rooms) doesn't quite pull off the funky European-hip concept they're going for but don't let that put you off. This place is a great find. Staff go out of their way to help and the decent-sized rooms - with their 'wall-graffiti' art theme - boast gleaming modern bathrooms. Breakfast included, Wi-Fi.

$$$ Hayete Guesthouse, Rue Furn El-Hayek (1st floor, above 'Frida' restaurant), Achrafieh, T70-271530, www.hayete-guesthouse.com. This quirkily cool guesthouse, right in the heart of Achrafieh, has just 4 individually decorated rooms on offer. It's a charming place with lashings of character, some of the original intricate floor tiles still in place and a cute communal balcony perfect for lazing around on. Unfortunately service can be haphazard. Breakfast included, Wi-Fi, reserve as far in advance as possible as it's often booked out.

$$$ Hotel Libanais, T03-513766, www.hotelibanais.com. For those who'd prefer something different, this small company offers a glimpse of Lebanese life with 2 B&B accommodation options in the city. It's a chance to experience the friendly and welcoming Lebanese in their own homes. Reservations (at least 48 hrs' notice) are required. Check their website for details.

$$$ La Maison de Hamra, Corner Rue Hamra and Rue Omar Ben Abdul Aziz, Hamra, T01-744344, www.lamaisondehamra.com. The suites here, complete with tiny kitchenette, are a good compromise if you don't fancy eating out every night. Behind a rather dingy maze of corridors, the huge rooms are modern, bright and minimally styled (though some of the bathrooms could do with an update). The central Hamra location is also a bonus though light-sleepers should be aware that road-noise is a problem throughout the hotel. Wi-Fi.

$$$ Le Commodore, Rue Commodore, Hamra, T01-734734, www.lecommodorehotel.com. Foreign journalists that stayed at the legendary Commodore during the civil war wouldn't recognize the place these days. This old dame of the Hamra scene (famous for managing to stay open in the midst of total bedlam) is now a classy top-end hotel. Well-appointed, comfortable rooms are tastefully decorated, come with all the usual mod cons and have lovely personal touches which give the place a homely feel. Restaurants, bars, shops, swimming pool, Wi-Fi, parking.

$$$ Mayflower, Rue Nehme Yafet, Hamra, T01-340680, www.mayflowerbeirut.com. Although rather blandly decorated, the decent-sized, sparkling clean rooms (some with balcony) are comfortably appointed with minibar, a/c and satellite TV. It's in a great position just down from busy Rue Hamra. Overall, a solid choice. Across the road is the **Napoleon Hotel** which offers pretty much the same deal. Pub, restaurant, small rooftop swimming pool, Wi-Fi.

$$ Cedarland, Rue Omar Ben Abdul Aziz, Hamra, T01-340233, www.cedarlandhotel.net. An excellent central location for a hotel in this price range. You don't get much, but the large clean rooms come with a/c and satellite TV as standard and some have balconies attached. The bathrooms could do with an update but they're decently sized. For this price we're not complaining. The downstairs coffee shop is a nice added touch. Wi-Fi.

$$ Embassy, Rue Makdissi, Hamra, T01-340814, www.embassyhotellebanon.com. The Embassy exudes old-fashioned, cosy charm with clean rooms (a/c, minibar, fridge, satellite TV) decked out in enough frills and chintz to make your grandma proud. Most have dinky balconies that look out onto the inner garden rather than the street. Staff here are a genuinely welcoming bunch. Restaurant, Wi-Fi.

$$ Port View, Rue Al Nahr (just off Rue Gouraud), Gemmayze, T01-567500, www.portviewhotel.com. A friendly place just a short stroll from Gemmayze's bar scene. The airy rooms (a/c, satellite TV) are large and clean and come with small, slightly run down bathrooms. Light sleepers should be aware that noise can be an issue. Breakfast included, Wi-Fi.

$$ Regis, just off Rue Ibn Sina, Hamra, T01-361845, www.regishotel-lb-com. A short stroll from the Corniche, the Regis is a home away from home. Upstairs the sparsely furnished rooms (a/c, satellite TV) are made bright and cheerful by colourful bedding. Downstairs it's more living room than foyer, with book exchange, squashy sofas and obliging manager Mazer, who is always ready to dish out information and advice. Wi-Fi. Highly recommended.

$$ University, Rue Bliss, Hamra, T01-365391. A simple and safe place to rest your head; the rooms here are nothing special but do come with a/c and satellite TV. Unfortunately competition for rooms is stiff due to this place being booked up by AUB students during term time but during term holidays you should get a room no problems. Wi-Fi.

$ CYC Guesthouse, Shatila Palestinian refugee camp (ask your service taxi driver to take you to Shatila and drop you at Sabre Hmadeh intersection; if you ring ahead the CYC staff can meet you here), T03-974672, www.cycshatila.org/guesthouse/. This wonderful initiative was set up as an income-generating project for the Shatila Children and Youth Centre (CYC), which runs after-school activities, tutoring and training programs for the youth living in the camp. Based in the same building as the CYC offices, the guesthouse has basic dorm accommodation (US$15) with a communal kitchen (fridge, washing machine, cooker) available for guests' use and a cheerful lounge with TV. There are absolutely no luxuries but it's all clean, incredibly friendly and is a wonderful opportunity for visitors to find out more about Palestinian life within the camps. There are copious opportunities to work as a volunteer here as well.

$ Pension Al-Nazih, Rue 62, just off Av Charles Helou, Gemmayze, T01-564868, www.pension-alnazih.8m.com. This cute place pulls the punters in with its cheerful clean rooms. Doubles have a/c, satellite TV and private bath while the 5-bed dorms (US$17), which share decent communal bathrooms, have fan and satellite TV. On a downside, staff can be surly and Wi-Fi isn't free.

$ Saifi Urban Gardens, Rue Pasteur (behind Coral Petrol St), Gemmayze,

T01-562509, www.saifigardens.com. Hands down the best budget choice in town, Saifi Urban Gardens manages to be a tranquil oasis while still being in the thick of the action. The high-ceilinged rooms are airy, bright and decently sized and even the 4-bed dorms (US$18), which are the roomiest in the city, have private bathrooms and a/c. There's a friendly café and buzzing rooftop bar as well. Breakfast included, discounted rates for long stays, Wi-Fi. Highly recommended.

🍴 Restaurants

Beirut *p20, maps p20, p30, p33 and p38*
If you've been hanging around the Middle East for a while, you'll probably descend on Beirut's dining scene like a thirsty man coming in from the desert. And if you've just flown in, you're going to be amazed at how cosmopolitan this city's restaurant-life is. Not only is this city home to some of the best Levantine cuisine in the region but, if you're feeling like a break from meze and other Arab staples, you'll have no problems tracking down restaurants specializing in French, Italian, Japanese, Indian, Chinese or basically any other world cuisine. The average cost of a meal out in Beirut is around US$20 and portions tend to be on the generous side.

Unfortunately if you're on a budget , all this indulging your taste buds doesn't come cheap. Luckily the city is full of hole-in-the-wall style bakeries, falafel and *shawarma* stands, where you can easily fill up for 5000 LBP or less. Excellent local chain outlets such as **Kabab-Ji** and **Barbar** dish up brilliant *shawarma*, while **Faysal** does a whole range of budget pastries and pizza and is open around the clock. A good place for cheap eats in Hamra is along Rue Bliss, opposite the AUB, where dozens of budget eateries line the street. In East Beirut there are also some great cheapies. Rue Gouraud in Gemmayze has **Fern Ghattas** for all your *mannoushi* (a sort of Middle Eastern pancake) needs, **Crew Hut** on Rue Armenia has a fantastic array of sandwiches and there are a couple of good falafel stores on Rue Furn El Hayek, opposite the ABC shopping mall. A patisserie/gelato store worth hunting out is **Taj al-Moulouk** on Rue Bliss in Hamra. The gelato they do here is particularly delicious, the service is great and at only 1500 LBP a scoop you can afford to indulge.

The distinction between restaurant, café and bar is pretty fluid in Beirut: many of the restaurants merge into bars complete with thumping music and dancing later in the evening, while most of the bars serve food with menus sometimes as extensive (and as good) as that in a restaurant.

$$$ Abdel Wahab, Rue Abdel Wahab el-Inglizi, Achrafieh, T01-200550. Daily 1200-2400. A great choice for sampling the typical Levantine cuisine this country is so famous for. If you can get a few people together, go crazy on the meze selection so you can check out as many of the dishes as possible.

$$$ Cru, Rue Makdessi, Hamra, T01-344565, Mon-Sat 1800-0100. The French-inspired menu, pared-down casual ambience and knowledgeable staff make Cru stand out in Hamra's crowded restaurant scene. If you're pining for a steak, this is the place to come. Their extensive (and reasonably priced) wine list also makes this the place in town to come to sample Lebanon's top tipples.

$$$ Maharajah, next to the Sporting Beach Club, off Av du General de Gaulle, Ain El Mreisse, T01-742275. Daily 1200-2400. Serving up generous portions of decent Indian cuisine, the grand dining room here has a great position looking over the Mediterranean.

$$$ Mayrig, 282 Rue Pasteur, Gemmayze, T01-572121. Daily 1200-2400. This cosy restaurant blends the spicy flavours of Armenian cuisine with some Levantine favourites. Don't leave without sampling the mante (Armenian ravioli) or the decadently rich cherry kebab.

$$$ Seza, Rue Patriarch Arida, off Rue Armenia, Mar Mikhael, T01-570711, Tue-Sun 1200-1700 and 2000-2400. Infused with buckets of French-bistro charm and an added smattering of oriental character, Seza has a romantic appeal that's hard to beat. Luckily the food lives up to the serenely stylish surroundings with a menu of tasty Armenian specialities.

$$$ Tawlet, Naher St, off Rue Armenia, Mar Mikhael, T01-448149. Mon-Fri 1300-1600, Sat 1200-1600. If you want to sample the best of Lebanese home cooking you really need to dine at Tawlet. More foodie experience than restaurant, an ever-changing band of home-cooks from across the country come here to cook their regional specialities. The lunchtime buffet is 50,000 LBP or you can opt for the dish of the day at 20,000 LBP. Highly recommended.

$$ Abou Hassan, Rue Salah ud-Din el-Ayoubi, Manara, T01-741725. Daily 0800-2200. Hidden away on a small street leading inland back towards Hamra and Ras Beirut, this small traditional Lebanese restaurant has a well-deserved reputation for serving excellent Arabic food at very reasonable prices. The pleasant atmosphere and friendly staff are a definite bonus. Recommended.

$$ Appetito Trattoria, Rue Mahatma Ghandi, Hamra, T01-347346. Daily 1200-2400. Super friendly service, a relaxed atmosphere and possibly the best pizza in town are the order of the day at this dinky Italian-style neighbourhood bistro. It's the sort of place where staff remember your name after one visit and everyone gets a free shot at the end of their meal. If you're in the mood for pasta or pizza this is the place to come. Recommended.

$$ Aunty Salwa, Baalbaki Building, off Rue Abdel Aziz, Hamra, T01-749746. Mon-Sat 0900-1700. Hearty home-style Lebanese dishes – the sort you don't find anywhere else. There's no menu, just whatever choices are being cooked that day. Recommended.

Eat your way through the city

Breakfast Have a modern take on a Lebanese breakfast at either Ginette or Bread Republic or grab a *kaak* (curious handbag-shaped bread stuffed with cheese or zaatar) at Fern Ghattas.
Mid-morning coffee For a caffeine pick-me-up head straight to Café Younis, home of Beirut's best coffee.
Lunch Social-empowerment enterprise and local foodie haven Tawlet is the place to eat lunch. Whatever is on the menu is bound to be good.
Mid-afternoon snack For the best *falafel* in town go to Falafel Sayhoun.
Dinner Dinner is late in Beirut. Reserve a table at either Mayrig or Seza to sample the cuisine of the city's Armenian community or for the full Lebanese experience feast on mezze at Abdel Wahab.

$ Falafel Sahyoun, Rue Bchara el Khoury, Downtown, T01-633188. This Beirut institution has been dishing up fried chickpea goodness since 1933 and is so famous Anthony Bourdain featured it on his 'No Reservations' TV show. Don't miss a falafel (3000 LBP) from here.
$ Le Chef, Rue Gouraud, Gemmayze, T01-445373. Mon-Sat 0700-2100. Welcome! Welcome! Welcome! This place is legendary for the hilarious antics of the owner who, if in the mood, booms out the word 'welcome' to you at least 20 times during the course of your meal. Yes, it's now a tourist trap and yes, the food can be so-so, but this unpretentious café is a cheerful and low-cost choice where you can eat for well less than US$10. Simple dishes (5000-8000 LBP) and meze (2000-6000 LBP) are all hearty and filling, and the hummus here is fantastic. A good fun, no-frills option. Recommended.
$ Zaatar w Zeit, Rue Bliss, Hamra; Rue Gouraud, Gemmayze. Cheap, filling, tasty and always packed, this local chain restaurant does its own delicious take on the staple *mannoushi* as well as offering all sorts of other pastry delights.

Cafés

Café culture is huge in Beirut. There are literally dozens of cafés in Hamra, especially along Rue Hamra and Rue Makdissi; all around East Beirut's Gemmayze and Achrafieh districts; and in Downtown there are loads of places to put your feet up on the streets radiating out from Place d'Etoile.
Bread Republic, in an alleyway off Rue Hamra, Hamra. Daily 0730-2400. A very cool Hamra café favoured by Beirut's bohemian set. The inside is tiny but there is great outdoor seating that spreads across the narrow alleyway. Coffee is ho-hum, but there is excellent lemonade, juices and cocktails. They're known for their menu of all-day breakfasts and their range of artisanal breads. Recommended.
Café Younes, Rue Nehme, Hamra; Rue Omar Ben Abdul Aziz, Hamra. Daily 0700-2400. Hands down, the best coffee in town. You'll probably smell the tantalizing wafts of freshly ground beans before you actually get here. Café Younes has been around since 1935 and is still going strong. For caffeine addicts, this is your Beirut home-from-home. They also do a delicious range of sandwiches. Recommended.
Captain's Cabin, Rue Makdissi, Hamra. Daily 1700-late. A totally unpretentious and dingy Hamra institution that gets packed out with a nice mix of university students and expats. There's a pool table, darts board and definitely no need to dress up in your finest.
City Café, Rue Sadat, Hamra. Daily 0700-2400. An oldie but a goody; City Café is a friendly joint with a devoted following of regulars who come here for the decent coffee, pastries and more substantial meals.

An excellent choice for breakfast.

Dar Bistro, Rue de Rome, Hamra. Daily 0800-2400. This arty place is like hanging out at a very cool friend's house; one who also happens to make a good cup of coffee, can rustle up a menu of Mediterranean-inspired dishes if you're hungry and has a bookshop on site. The garden, complete with pastel-coloured furniture, is a chilled-out retreat from the city streets. Recommended.

Ginette, Rue Gouraud, Gemmayze. This design store and café combo has good coffee, on-the-ball service and a lovely outdoor patio. If you're peckish the menu dishes up seriously good breakfasts, healthy salads and a range of sandwiches.

Paul's, Rue Gouraud, Gemmayze. This café is the see-and-be-seen spot for Beirut's chi-chi set who come here for the excellent coffee and great range of pastries and breads that are baked on site. The downside is that the outdoor terrace is blighted by constant traffic and construction noise and staff can be off-hand if you don't arrive crimped and coiffed in your SUV.

🎵 Bars and clubs

Beirut *p20, maps p20, p30, p33 and p38*
Bars
Beirut's nightlife is alive and kicking with something for everyone. The 'in' places change regularly, with fickle crowds migrating somewhere new at rapid speed. The main nightlife areas are Hamra and Gemmayze. In Hamra bars are spread throughout the district with the area around Rue Makdissi having the biggest choice of options. In Gemmayze the nightlife scene begins on Rue Gouraud (and the small streets leading off it) but recently many new bars are popping up a little further east along Rue Armenia. No places really get going until after 2300.

A couple of things to note: many of the more upscale places (especially in Gemmayze) have cover charges, but you often won't be charged as you arrive. Instead you'll be charged on your final bill. Also, on bar menus all over Beirut (and Lebanon) you'll see 'Mexican beer' for sale. This is not a bottle of Corona, but a rather sickly concoction of almaza beer with lemon juice added to the glass and with the glass rim coated in salt. You'll either love it or hate it!

Barometre, Rue Makhoul, Hamra, T01-367229. Daily 1900-late. Immensely popular, Barometre is a hip spot where a cool mix of locals hang out for the great music (a blend of Arabic pop and Latin) and excellent food. They do a delicious range of meze options, so it's a good choice for a whole night of drinking, eating and dancing. If you want to get a seat, come here early as it gets jam-packed as the night progresses. Despite the lack of space, patrons break out their dance moves later on in the evening, strutting their stuff between the tables and chairs. A great, fun bar. Recommended.

Behind the Green Door, Rue Armenia, just off Rue Gouraud, Gemmayze, T01-565656. Daily 2000-late. Beirut does ostentatious well, and this bar, with its opulent draperies and decorations and patronized by the la-di-dah boys and girls of Beirut high society, sums it up pretty well. Absolutely brilliant for people-watching and seeing how the other half live. Dress up, and plan on it being an expensive night. Reservations recommended.

Coop d'Etat, Saifi Urban Gardens, Rue Pasteur, Gemmayze, T71-134173. Daily 1800 0100. This rooftop bar is a fun and friendly choice that attracts a mixed crowd of artsy locals, ex-pats and travellers (many staying at Saifi Urban Gardens downstairs). They often host special events and there's always good food and music.

Dany's, The Alleyway, off Rue Makdissi, Hamra, T01-740231. Daily 1100-late. With walls covered in graffiti, good music, friendly service and decently priced beer, Dany's is a godsend for anyone tired of Beirut's see-and-be-seen nightlife. Happy hour (usually 1700-2000) offers half-price cocktails and super-cheap beer and there's regular live music. It gets quite a squeeze in here later on so come before 2200 if you want to grab a table. Recommended.

February 30, The Alleyway, off Rue Makdissi, Hamra, T76-994405. Daily 1000-0400. An extensive cocktail list and kitch decoration that's part vintage Americana and part mannequin factory raid has made February 30 a favourite of Hamra's cool young set. It buzzes most nights of the week.

Godot, Rue Gouraud, Gemmayze, T01-575770. Daily 1600-0200. Our favourite Gemmayze drinking spot is a sliver of a place with a mean range of cocktails, super friendly staff, and a great range of music at a decibel level where you don't have to shout. The decor has an arty vibe and the crowd verges this way too. Recommended.

Main Street, Rue Uruguay, Downtown, T76-090953; Rue Makdissi, Hamra T76-680674. Daily 1700-0200. A friendly place that has live DJs later on in the night (when it can get really crowded). Earlier on it's more relaxed and the happy hour prices (from 1700-2000) make it a good choice to start out the night.

Pacifico, Monot Alley, Monot, Achrafieh, T01-204446. Daily 1900-late. With a bit of Latin American style going on, popular Pacifico is a fun place for cocktails and dancing to the Cuban beats. If you want to eat (the Mexican-inspired menu is delicious and there are lots of snacky options) be sure to reserve a table as this place gets packed. Happy hour 1900-2000.

Rabbit Hole, Rue Makdissi, Hamra. Daily 1500-late. Anyone short of cash should make note of Rabbit Hole's daily happy hour, between 1700-2000, when their cheap and cheerful cocktails (obviously on the watered-down side) only cost 3000 LBP. With prices like that, it's no wonder this itsy-bitsy bar continues to be a popular spot to start out a night on the town.

Torino Express, Rue Gouraud, Gemmayze. Daily 1200-late. The original Gemmayze bar, Torino is still going strong and is as popular as ever. During the day this teensy place is a good spot to grab a coffee while in the evening it transforms into a friendly bar with a mixed bag of music and a nice crowd. A top spot though it can get ridiculously packed later on.

Clubs and live music

BO18, off Av Charles Helou (adjacent to the landmark Forum de Beyrouth), T01-580018. Thu-Sat 2100-late. BO18 (that's pronounced 'Bee Oh Eighteen') is Beirut's prime venue for debauchery and serious dancing action. Housed in a massive underground bunker with black leather couches lining the walls, this place attracts a huge cross section of Beiruti clubbers, but definitely verges on the alternative side. The prime feature is the retractable roof which is opened up as the night draws on. Despite the overpriced drinks and the cover charge, this place is not to be missed if you're a clubber.

Blue Note, Rue Makhoul, Hamra, T01-743857. Mon-Sat 1200-late. Live music fans will love the changing line up of live jazz bands on Fri and Sat nights. There are sometimes blues and rock acts as well. It's an unpretentious joint with a decent dinner menu. A minimum charge applies on Fri and Sat nights.

DRM (Democratic Republic of Music), Rue Sourati, Hamra, T01-752202, www.drmlebanon.com, 1930-late. This venue is a hub for both local and international musicians to play concerts. To see upcoming events, and buy tickets, check out the website.

Sky Bar, Biel Pavillion, Downtown, T03-939191, www.sky-bar.com. Summer months only, Tue-Sun 2030-late. Beirut's most talked about venue, the roof terrace Sky Bar is the city's see-and-be-seen venue of choice on balmy summer evenings. With an exclusive reputation to keep up, this place charges a minimum rate of US$100 per person if you want to sit at a table (yes you did read that right) and you'll need to make a reservation beforehand. A slightly less wallet-bashing way to experience the over-the-top decadence of Beirut's glitterati is to queue up for a place at the bar. Dress to impress.

🔊 Entertainment

Beirut *p20, maps p20, p30, p33 and p38*
Children
Beirut Luna Park, Av du General de Gaulle. The original Beirut fairground, with funky dodgem cars and a retro ferris wheel.
Planet Discovery, Souk Ayyas, Beirut Souks, Downtown, T01-980650, www. solidere.com/beirut-souks/planet-discovery, Mon-Fri 0830-1800, Sat-Sun 1030-1900. Described as a 'children's science museum', there are lots of different activities and interactive games for children here, from age 3 through to 15. There are puppet shows every Sat and craft workshops throughout the week.

Cinema
The *Daily Star* newspaper has cinema listings.
Art Lounge, Karantina River Bridge, near Beirut Forum, Karantina, T03-997676, www. artlounge.net. Art house and alternative films shown every Sun. See their website for details on what's screening.
Empire Sodeco, Sodeco Sq, Achrafieh, T01-616707. Popular multiplex showing all the latest Hollywood blockbusters.
Grand ABC, ABC Mall, Rue Achrafieh, Achrafieh, T01-209109. Always busy, this multiplex has 7-screens to choose from.

Galleries
Beirut's art scene is booming. There are dozens of small galleries around town exhibiting young emerging local artists as well as international names.
Agial, Rue Abdel Aziz, Hamra, www.agialart. com. Mon-Fri 1000-1800, Sat 1000-1400. A huge range of Middle Eastern artists are represented in this 2-levelled gallery. Upstairs is the permanent collection, while the ground floor plays host to a regular turn-over of exhibitions. One of the best places in town to check out the local art scene.

Alice Mogabgab, 1st floor, Karam Building, Rue Achrafieh, Achrafieh, www. alicemogabgab.com. Mon-Sat 1000--1900 (Aug and Sep by appointment only). An impressive collection of local and international modern art is on display here.
Art Lounge, Karantina River Bridge, near Beirut Forum, Karantina, www. artlounge.net. This funky space focuses on young local artists and has a program of changing exhibitions. Also weekly cinema nights (see above) and various other cultural events.
Ayyam, ground floor, Beirut Tower, Corniche, Downtown, T01-374450, www. ayyamgallery.com. Mon-Sat 1000-2000. Opened in 2009, this gallery is dedicated to showcasing contemporary work by artists from all over the Arab world.
Beirut Exhibition Center, off Rue Allenby, Beirut Waterfront, T01-962000, www. beirutexhibitioncenter.com, daily 1100-2000. The BEC hosts a range of temporary exhibitions from retrospectives on big name local artists to international shows.

Theatres
Al Medina, Rue Clemenceau, Hamra, T01-753011, www.almadinatheatre.com. Has an ever-changing program of theatre, dance and other cultural productions. Tickets can be bought on site.
Monot, Rue University of St Joseph, adjacent to St Joseph's Church, Monot, T01-202422. Wide variety of performances (dance, music and theatre).Tickets sold on site.

✸ Festivals and events

Beirut *p20, maps p20, p30, p33 and p38*
Apr Beirut International Platform of Dance, www.maqamat.org, this dance festival attracts a host of international dance companies as well as local performers.
May Spring Festival, a 5-day garden show event that turns the city's Hippodrome into a floral extravaganza.

Jun Fete de la Musique, began in Beirut in 1982, this is a celebration of world music that plays at various venues throughout the capital, and in the streets of Downtown, Hamra and Gemmayzeh. The festival takes place over the summer solstice.

Jun Gemmaze Stairs Art Festival, this wonderful local art carnival utilizes the length of the St Nicholas stairs, turning the entire stairway into a unique gallery space. It's an original and quirky way to bring art to the people and both international artists and complete amateurs can exhibit.

Jul-Aug Lebanese Film Festival, www. neabeyrouth.org, one of the best chances visitors have to catch the cinematic offerings of local film makers.

Oct-Nov Beirut International Film Festival, www.beirutfilmfoundation.org, one of the Middle East's premier film festivals; Beirut plays host to the best cinema offerings from across the globe.

Nov Beirut International Marathon, www. beirutmarathon.org, taking over the streets of Beirut, runners from all across the globe compete in this annual event.

○ Shopping

Beirut *p20, maps p20, p30, p33 and p38*
Books

Beirut has some excellent bookshops. Most stock a wide range of books in English and French as well as Arabic, and a startling array of international magazines and newspapers (though prices aren't particularly cheap).

El Bourj, ground floor of An Nahar Building, just off Martyr's Sq, Downtown. Fantastic collection of books on Lebanon and the Middle East.

Librairie Antoine, Rue Hamra, Hamra. An absolutely huge selection of international magazines and newspapers and downstairs there is a vast array of books in English and French, with Lebanese and Middle Eastern authors well represented and a decent politics/history section.

Librairie Orientale, Rue Hamra, Hamra. Large collection of books in English, French and Arabic, including a good range of fiction by Arabic authors. Also, coffee table books on Lebanon and travel books.

Virgin Megastore, Martyr's Sq, Downtown and ABC Mall, Achrafieh. The massive Virgin store carries a wide range of titles as well as lots of glossy magazines. The travel section here is the best in the city, the history and politics section is pretty good and the range of novels is excellent. The smaller branch in Achrafieh doesn't have as much choice.

Way Inn, Rue Hamra, Hamra. An eclectic mix of books, stationery and international magazines and newspapers. There is a decent range of books focusing on Middle Eastern history and politics with some fiction thrown in.

Handicrafts, antiques and souvenirs

Compared to other Middle Eastern cities, the prices of handicrafts in Beirut are high, but in general so is the quality.

There are numerous souvenir/antique shops in Hamra, along and in the streets radiating off Rue Hamra. In Achrafieh there are numerous antique shops, most of them specializing in elegant furniture and furnishings along the lines of reproduction Louis XIV items, but there are also lots of places selling smaller items such as jewellery. Rue Achrafieh is a good street to browse in. The artist's quarter of **Saifi village** is home to plenty of boutique gift stores.

Artisans du Liban et d'Orient, Rue Minet el-Hosn, Ain el-Mreisse. Mon-Fri 1000-1800, Sat 1000-1330. Interesting selection of handicrafts and local produce including hand-woven rugs, fabrics, glassware, soaps, spices and some books.

Hassan Maktabi & Sons, Av General de Gaulle, Raouche. Mon-Sat 0930-1800. A highly reputable carpet dealership with an absolutely huge selection of Central Asian carpets and *kilims* (Persian, Turkish, Caucasian and Nomadic).

naash, 1st floor, Bikhaazi and Cherif Building, off Rue Sidani, Hamra, www.inaash.org. Mon-Fri 0800-1500, Sat 0800-1300. Showroom for the work created by the women employed by the Association for Palestinian Embroidery in Lebanon. Employing over 450 female Palestinian refugees, this project not only provides the women with money but also makes sure that the traditional designs of Palestinian embroidery are kept alive.

Maison De L'Artisan, Rue Minet el-Hosn, Ain el-Mreisse. Mon-Sat 0930-2000. Large government-sponsored shop displaying a wide range of souvenirs and traditional handicrafts from all over Lebanon: ceramics, tapestries, woven rugs, silver jewellery, *narghiles*, pottery, metal-ware, cutlery, glassware, inlaid wood items, fabrics, etc.

Souk El-Tayeb, Sat 0900-1400, Rue Trablous, Beirut Souks, Downtown (BCD). Bringing the countryside to the city, Souk El-Tayeb gives farmers from all over Lebanon a platform to sell their products. A must-do for foodies with an excellent range of local, organic produce for sale.

◐ What to do

Beirut *p20, maps p20, p30, p33 and p38*
Beach clubs
The term 'Beach Club' is something of a misnomer, since there are only a couple of real sand beaches in Beirut. For most Lebanese, however, the absence of any beach at their favourite beach club is neither here nor there. What's important is that it's a club, a private place for relaxing, socializing and enjoying a sense of exclusivity (though these days the majority are open to the public for a straightforward entrance fee). Be warned, turning up at most of these clubs without a tanned and toned body is verging on the subversive. Starting at the new **Zaitunay Bay** marina complex and following the coast west and then south, the main clubs are in the following order:

St George's Yacht Club, Rue Minet el-Hosn (The Corniche), T01-327 050. Mon-Fri 20,000 LBP, child 15,000 LBP; Sat-Sun 35,000 LBP, child 20,000 LBP. Formerly, this was a luxury hotel with its own private beach club and marina but, like most of the hotels and restaurants in this area, St George's was devastated during the civil war. The large hotel building still stands in a state of ruin (there is a long-standing legal battle between the owners and Solidere, with the latter claiming ownership of the land/sea frontage as part of the redevelopment area), but the adjoining beach club is as popular as ever among wealthy Beirutis. Facilities include a swimming pool, waterslide, children's play area, restaurant, three bars, a small marina for motor yachts, jet skis for hire and a privately run diving club. During the summer, evening entertainments are often laid on (singers, bands, dancing, etc).

Ajram Beach, Rue Minet el-Hosn. T01-374753, 10,000 LBP. The city's first women-only beach club is still going strong. Rather basic facilities compared to other clubs.

AUB Beach, Corniche, non-AUB students 10,000 LBP. Reached via a tunnel from the university grounds, this is a less well-maintained beach than others along the Corniche but a fun and friendly place to spend an afternoon sunbathing.

Riviera Beach Club, Corniche, T01-373210, Mon-Fri 30,000 LBP, Sat-Sun 40,000 LBP, child 25,000. Nicknamed 'silicone beach' for a reason, this highly prestigious beach club does nothing by halves, with swimming pool, health centre (with jacuzzi, sauna, massage and gym), as well as a restaurant and bar. This isn't the place for showcasing your old pair of boardies and tired flip flops.

Sporting Beach Club, Corniche, T01-742200, Mon-Sun 25,000 LBP. Strong family emphasis, with 2 large swimming pools and children's pool, large concrete sunbathing area and steps down to the sea. Restaurants.

Rafiq Hariri Beach, to the south of Raouche heading down towards the Summerland and Coral Beach hotels, free public beach.

As well as having a decent stretch of sand that's kept relatively clean, a sectioned-off swimming area, snack bar and basic shower and changing facilities, this beach has the advantage of being open to the general public with no entrance fee required.

Diving
Water Nation, Zaitunay Bay, Beirut Marina, T01-379770, www.waternation.com.lb. As well as diving courses from beginner to technical, Water Nation offers a myriad of water sports including boat and jet-ski rental, water skiing and parasailing.

Spas and beauty
You really can't pretend to be a Beiruti unless you're properly primped and preened, and you won't have any problems finding a place to pluck those eyebrows or buff those nails.
Jessy's, off Rue Nehme Yafet, Hamra. A small, unpretentious joint offering a full range of beauty treatments at extremely reasonable prices. Recommended.
Naiiman, Rue Verdun, T01-787858, www.naiiman.com. Trendy nail and hair salon with a popular male barbershop on site as well.
Salon Younes Eid, 1st floor, Starco Building, Downtown. Totally luxurious and exclusive, this high-class hair and beauty salon is frequented by Beirut's glitterati who come here for their pampering. Offers a full range of beauty services.

Sports
Beirut By Bike, Rue Al Mreisse, Ain Mreisse, T01 365524, www.beirutbybike.com. For those brave enough to take Beirut's traffic on, Beirut By Bike rent out cycles by the day.
Cyclosport, Rue Gouraud, Gemmayze, T01-446792, www.cyclosportlb.com. Daily 1030-2100. This cycle shop rents out bikes by the hour (5000 LBP) or on a 24-hr (25,000 LBP) basis. They also sell bikes and are a great point of call if you need your own fixed.

Golf Club of Lebanon, between Blvd Ouzai and New Airport Highway, Bourj Brajneh, T01-826335, www.golfclub.org.lb, daily 0730-1930. An 18-hole course that's been keeping Beirut's golfers happy since 1923. Excellent facilities: gym, swimming pool, tennis and squash courts, pub and restaurant. Golf equipment for rent.
Hash House Harriers, http://www.geocities.com/beiruttarboush/. The Beirut chapter of the famous 'drinking club with a running problem' hosts regular runs (and walks) every 2nd Sun afternoon, and every full moon night, throughout the year. They also sometimes organize other events.
Hippodrome, near the National Museum, T01-632515, www.beiruthorseracing.com. For those who like to take a punt, the Hippodrome hosts horse racing once a week throughout the year with the day's racing taking place every Sun right through Sep-Jun (starting 1230) and on Sat during Jul-Aug (starting 1330). There are 8 races throughout the day with 10-12 horses taking part in every race.

⊖ Transport

Beirut *p20, maps p20, p30, p33 and p38*
Air
Rafiq Hariri International Airport, T01-628 195, www.beirutairport.gov.lb, is around 10 km to the south of the city centre. By far the easiest way to get to the airport is by taxi, and the going rate for tourists is US$20. If you don't feel like haggling, book a taxi beforehand. To get to the airport on a budget, catch the **LCC No 5 bus**, which begins on Av General De Gaulle in Ain el-Mreisse , in West Beirut, and passes through Cola Junction, or **LCC No A bus**, which begins at Dora Junction on the Antelias Highway in East Beirut and passes by Martyrs' Square (45 mins, 1000 LBP). Both will drop you off at the roundabout 1 km away from the airport complex. If you've got lots of luggage you're better off taking a taxi.

Rafiq Hariri is the main hub for **Middle East Airlines (MEA)**, T01-622000, www.mea.com.lb, which also has an office in the Gefinor Centre in Hamra, T01-622225. MEA operate regular flights to **Amman**, **Amsterdam**, **Athens**, **Cairo**, **Chicago**, **Copenhagen**, **Dubai**, **Frankfurt**, **Geneva**, **Istanbul**, **London**, **Los Angeles**, **Madrid**, **Montreal**, **New York**, **Paris**, **Rome** and **Toronto**, among others. Flights to North America have a stopover in either Paris or London.

Other airlines that fly out of Beirut include **Air France** (T01-977977, www.airfrance.fr), **British Airways** (T01-747777), **Egypt Air** (T01-629356, www.egyptair.com), **Emirates** (T01-734500, www.emirates.com), **Etihad** (T01-975000, www.etihadairways.com), **Gulf Air** (T01-323332, www.gulfair.com), **Lufthansa** (T01-347005, www.lufthansa.com), **Pegasus Airlines** (www.flypgs.com), **Royal Jordanian** (T01-379990, www.rj.com) and **Turkish Airlines** (T01-999849, www.turkishairlines.com). Departure tax is usually included in your flight ticket.

Bus

Local Although the local bus system can be tricky, there are some bus routes that are useful for visitors. The local Lebanese Commuting Company (LCC) buses are red and white and display their route number prominently on the front windscreen. Ticket prices are always either 1000 LBP or 1500 LBP. You can hail them down and get off them anywhere along the route. If you have no idea when to get off, just tell the driver your destination and he'll let you know. Some handy bus routes are listed below:

LCC Bus No 1 Hamra to Khalde: Begins in Hamra on Rue Sadat, passing Rue Verdun, Cola Junction and Kafaat before finishing in Khalde.

LCC Bus No 2 Hamra to Antelias: Begins in Hamra on Rue Emile Edde, passing Sassine Sq in Achrafieh, Mar Mikhael, Bourj Hammoud and Dora Junction before finishing in Antelias.

LCC Bus No 5 Manara to Hay as-Saloum: Begins in Manara on Av General De Gaulle pasing Verdun and the international airport before finishing in Hay as-Saloum.

LCC Bus No 6 Cola Junction to Byblos: Begins at Cola Junction before passing through Dora Junction, Antelias, Kaslik and Jounieh before finishing in Byblos. This bus heads straight down the Antelias highway so it's also a great option for travelling to the Cilicia Museum on a budget.

LCC Bus No 8 Hamra to Ain Saadeh: Begins on Rue Sidani in Hamra and passes Sassine Sq in Achrafieh and Bourj Hammoud before finishing in Ain Saadeh. It'll get you to the Armenian district of Bourj Hammoud.

Long distance There are 2 main bus stations in Beirut. **Charles Helou bus station**, underneath an elevated section of Av Charles Helou, just to the east of the port area, deals with transport heading north and also transport heading to **Syria**, while **Cola Junction bus station** isn't really a bus station at all and is just a transport hub spread around a large, chaotic roundabout underneath a flyover to the southwest of the centre. It deals with all transport heading south and to the **Bekaa Valley**.

Charles Helou bus station is divided into sections. **Zone B** is for buses to **Tripoli** (1½ hrs). There are 2 companies operating comfortable a/c buses from here. **Connexion** run buses every 15 mins between 0730-1900 (4000 LBP). **Tripoli Express** buses are slightly older and leave every 30 mins or so (3000 LBP). You can jump off the bus at any point along the northern highway, but you'll be charged the full price to Tripoli. There are also plenty of **minibuses** heading north to Tripoli that congregate at the eastern side of the station (nearer Zone A). If you're heading to **Byblos**, **Batroun** or another town on the way to Tripoli this is a slightly cheaper option than the buses (usually 2000 LBP).

Zone A is for **international departures**. From here **service taxis** head to **Damascus** (3 hrs, 3000 SYP). Please be aware that although transport is still running to **Syria**, travelling there at the current time is not only unadvisable due to the ongoing conflict but is discouraged by most governmental travel advisories.

Cola Junction bus station has a mixture of buses, minibuses and service taxis operating from it, primarily to destinations to the south of Beirut but also to the **Bekaa Valley**. From the west side of the roundabout there are regular **minibuses** to **Sidon** (1 hr, 2000 LBP) and **Chtaura** (1 hr, 4000 LBP). The buses to Chtaura often carry on to **Zahle** (1¼ hrs, 5000 LBP) and then **Baalbek** (2 hrs, 6000 LBP). If not, you can easily swap buses in Chtaura. There are also less regular minibuses to **Nabatiye** (1 hr, 5000 LBP).

This is also where you can get a **service taxi** to **Sidon** (45 mins, 5000 LBP) and **Tyre** (1½ hrs, 10,000 LBP). These taxis leave quite regularly during the morning hours. Much less frequent are service taxis to **Beiteddine** (45 mins, 10,000 LBP) and to **Chtaura** (45 mins, 10,000 LBP). These only leave if enough passengers turn up so come early for your best chance.

If you can't get a service taxi to Beiteddine, a **minibus** to the **Chouf** leaves from just north of the main service taxi/minibus stand. Keeping the flyover on your right, cross the road from the main bus stand and walk 2 blocks up the road. The bus leaves regularly from a small unsigned parking space just after the Hafez Motors building and just before the road intersection. This bus passes by the road junction a short walk from **Beiteddine** itself (1 hr, 2500 LBP).

The eastern side of the roundabout is the starting point for the **LCC No 6 bus** to **Byblos** (1½ hrs, 1500 LBP). If you are heading anywhere along the north coast up to Byblos this bus is a great option as it takes the old coast highway so that you can be dropped inside the towns rather than on the highway.

As well as the above main 2 transport hubs, at **Dora Junction** on the Antelias highway, past Bourj Hammoud, you can pick up any of the transport heading north from Charles Helou bus station. On **Rue Badaro** just south of the National Museum ('*Mathaf*' in Arabic) you can catch **LCC bus No 7** to **Beit Meri** and **Broummana** in Mount Lebanon.

Car hire
Avis, Airport, T01-629890; Downtown (Phoenicia Intercontinental Hotel), T01-762626; www.avis.com.lb.
Budget, Airport, T01-629891; Rue Clemenceau, Hamra,T01-360847; www.budget.com.
Hala Rent-a-car, Airport, T01-629444; Rue Sami el Sohl, Achrafieh, T01-393904; www.halacar.com.
Lenacar/Europcar, Airport, T01-629888; www.europcarlebanon.com.
Hertz, Airport, T01-628998; www.hertz.com.
Sixt Rent-a-car, Corniche el-Mazraa, T01-301226, www.sixt.com.lb.

Service taxis and private taxis
See also page 22.

Although many Beirut taxis don't have a 'taxi' sign on their roof, you can spot a service/private taxi by its number plates. All taxis must have red number plates to distinguish them from private vehicles.

Service (shared) taxis are the most popular form of local transport in Beirut. They simply head for the destination of their first passenger and then look for more customers along the way.

The standard price of a service taxi ride anywhere within the city is 2000 LBP but if the driver wasn't going that way, or thinks your destination is too far away he may say '*serveece-ain*' ('double service'), which costs 4000 LBP. There is no rhyme or reason to this pricing; it's up to the discretion of the individual taxi driver. If you don't want to pay double the price, wait for the next taxi to come along; he may be happy to only charge you a single fare. Always confirm that the taxi is operating as a service taxi ('*serveece*') before getting in.

Getting to grips with the system takes some time. It helps to position yourself along a major road heading in the overall direction that you wish to go, bearing in mind the 1-way system. Thus, to head east from Hamra, you need to be on Rue Emile Edde/Rue Spears; service taxis running along Rue Hamra will all take you out towards Manara and Raouche.

Most of the service taxis will also operate as private taxis if you want. The standard rate for a journey inside the city is 10,000 LBP, though for some shorter trips you may only be charged 5000-6000 LBP. Always agree on a price before getting into the taxi. Late at night you can expect to pay double. If you don't want to hail a taxi on the street, most hotels can book a taxi to pick you up.

All the below taxis can be booked for half and full-day sightseeing journeys throughout the country as well as for shorter trips within the city itself: **Alfa Taxi**, T01-560910; **Allo Taxi**, T01-366661; **Charlie Taxi**, T01-265205.

ℹ Directory

Beirut *p20, maps p20, p30, p33 and p38*
Cultural centres The foreign cultural centres in Beirut are primarily geared towards providing language courses and information on their respective countries for the Lebanese, but are also of interest to tourists for their newspapers and magazines, film nights, cultural programmes and occasional lectures. Always take your passport along if you want to access a centre. The French centre is the most active. **British Council**, Berytech Building, Rue de Damas, T01-428900, www. britishcouncil.org/lebanon, Mon-Fri 0900-1800. Has a small library and organizes art exhibitions, film showings and theatre events. **French Cultural Centre (CCF)**, Rue de Damas (near the National Museum),

T01-420230, www.ambafrance-liban.org. lb. Has a monthly program of events and art exhibitions, hosts regular film nights and boasts a large library. **Goethe Institute**, Rue Nahr Ibrahim, T01-446092, www.goethe. de/beirut. Has a varied program of lectures, events, exhibitions and concerts as well as a good library. **Instituto Cervantes**, Rue Maarad, Downtown, T01-970253, www. cervantes.es. There is a decent library here and the centre hosts occasional exhibitions and events. **Language courses** Centre for Arab and Middle Eastern Studies (CAMES), American University of Beirut, T01-350000, www.aub.edu.lb. Every summer CAMES runs an extremely well regarded, 8-week, intensive Arabic language program with 7 levels of study to choose from. It's a demanding course and not cheap (course fees are US$4050), but if you're serious about studying Arabic this is an excellent option. Classes generally run Mon-Fri for 6 hrs per day. Applications to enrol in the course must be made by Mar and details can be found on their website. **Saifi Institute**, Rue Pasteur, Gemmayze, T01-560738, www.saifiarabic.com. This private language centre runs a range of courses throughout the year specializing in teaching practical day-to-day Arabic skills. Course levels cater for the complete novice to the advanced speaker and cost between US$240-600 dependent on how intensive your course is. Accommodation is available for students at Saifi Urban Gardens, which is based in the same building and run by the same people. Highly recommended by expats living in Beirut. **Medical services** There are numerous private hospitals dotted around Beirut. The **American University Hospital (AUH)**, Rue Omar Ben Abdul Aziz, Hamra, T01-350000, is centrally located and has excellent facilities as well as a well stocked pharmacy. There are dozens of good pharmacies throughout the city.

Contents

Footprint features

Around Beirut

North from Beirut

Don't judge a book by its cover. Concealed behind the sprawl of high-rises that dominate this stretch of coast are some fantastic sights. Byblos, with its pretty harbourside souq and important archaeological site, is the main north coast highlight but even ugly-looking Jounieh, with its hideous concrete calamities, has an Ottoman-period heart hiding some charming buildings from that era. Thrill-seekers shouldn't miss a ride on the terrifying Jounieh teleferique, while those who like a flutter will enjoy a night out at the casino. Just out of town is the Jeita Grotto, which makes a pleasant half-day trip from Beirut or Jounieh, or a full-day excursion when combined with Byblos.

Jeita Grotto → *For listings, see pages 67-70.*

Not to be missed, the enormous Jeita Grotto contains one of the largest collections of stalactites and stalagmites in the world. The formations are a breathtakingly beautiful example of the forces of nature and time at work. The grotto in fact consists of an upper and lower network of caverns that together extend for more than 6 km into the mountainside.

It was first discovered in 1836 by Reverend Thomas, an American who was living in Beirut. Sheltering in a cave while out on a hunting trip, he heard the sound of running water coming from inside. Firing his gun into the cave he realized its size and reported his find to the authorities in Beirut. It was not until 1873 that a team from the Beirut Water Supply Company explored further. They established that this was one of the major sources of the Nahr el-Kalb river. With its substantial output, the spring was subsequently used as a source for Beirut's water supply.

Further explorations, carried out in the early part of last century, culminated in the discovery of the upper network of caverns in 1958. In 1969 the caverns were opened to the public as a tourist attraction for the first time and became an instant hit. During the civil war, Jeita was used as a weapons and ammunition store by some of the Christian militias and wasn't opened to the public again until 1995. Jeita remains, today, an immensely popular tourist attraction; if you're here in July or August, try to avoid visiting on weekends, as it will be packed full of sightseers.

Arriving at Jeita Grotto
Getting there and away There's no public transport to the grotto. However, you can take any northbound bus, minibus or service taxi from Charles Helou bus station in Beirut and ask to be dropped at the Jeita Grotto turning. From there you'll have to walk 5 km to the entrance or negotiate with a private taxi. A much easier option is to take a taxi from Jounieh. A return journey to the grotto shouldn't cost more than US$20.

If you're driving from Beirut, head north on the coastal motorway and 1 km after passing through the tunnel at Nahr el-Kalb, take the exit signposted clearly for Ajaaltoun, and less clearly for Jeita Grotto. If you're coming from Jounieh (heading south along the motorway), there is an exit and bridge across the motorway. After a little over 3 km there is a right turn signposted for Jeita Grotto. This side road winds its way down into the picturesque Nahr el-Kalb Valley to arrive at the entrance to Jeita, 2.5 km away.

Visiting the grotto

ⓘ T09-220840, www.jeitagrotto.com, Tue-Sun 0900-1700, closed for 4 weeks from 7 Jan each year, 18,150 LBP, under 12-years 10,175 LBP, photography is officially banned inside the caverns.

A somewhat unnecessary cable car takes you the short distance from the main ticket office to the entrance to the upper grotto. By the entrance there is a theatre showing a 20-minute film giving good explanations of how the caverns and rock formations evolved (English-language versions at 0930, 1330 and 1730; French at 1130 and 1530).

A long tunnel complete with sound effects leads into the upper grotto. A concrete path runs for around 800 m through an awesome network of huge caverns, atmospherically lit and brimming with the most spectacular stalactites and stalagmites imaginable, including one stalactite which, at 7 m, is said to be the longest in the world. In places the stalactites hanging down from the roof have joined with the stalagmites rising from the floor to form solid columns. Elsewhere, the steady seepage of calcium carbonate-rich water through the limestone rock over millions of years has created all manner of weird and wonderful formations. The temperature here remains at a steady 22°C.

While the cable car taking you to the entrance to the upper grotto seems a little pointless, the miniature 'train' that takes you to the entrance to the lower grotto is downright silly. Once inside, a motorized boat, expertly manoeuvred by its skipper, takes you through the water-filled caverns (here the temperature is 16°C all year round). In comparison with the upper grotto, the lower one is perhaps not as spectacular, though it is still extremely impressive.

Jounieh → For listings, see pages 67 70.

A hodge-podge of high-rises, Jounieh is Lebanon at its brightest and brashest. It's hard to believe it looking at the ugly sprawl of concrete now, but before the civil war this was just a sleepy Christian port in the shadow of Beirut. With the fighting raging on in the capital, much of East Beirut's nightlife relocated here to create a world of hedonistic escapism for the privileged among Lebanon's Christian community, and quiet little Jounieh became the focus of a mad frenzy of development. What you see today is the result: a town built free from any urban-planning constraints; a mass of helter-skelter concrete towers squeezed between the broad sweep of the bay and the mountains.

Despite all the development, Jounieh has managed to retain some of its previous charm. The compact centre of town on the coast road has preserved a number of Ottoman-era buildings that now sit incongruously below the modern jumble of buildings above.

Jounieh remains a party town today. This is the home of the Casino du Liban, so if you want to burn a hole in your pocket, put your glad rags on and have a punt. The teleferique (cable car) to Harissa, on the hill above, is enjoyable (as long as you have a head for heights).

Arriving in Jounieh

Getting there and away All the buses and minibuses heading north from Beirut's Charles Helou bus station pass through Jounieh and can drop you on the highway as you pass through town. From there, walk down towards the coast to reach the town centre. The LCC No 6 Bus, which leaves from Cola Junction bus station, takes much longer but can drop you right in Jounieh's town centre on Rue Mina al-Jadida (at the roundabout next to KFC). If you're coming back to Beirut on this bus, make sure you wait on the northern stretch of this road before the roundabout as this is where the bus turns to re-join the motorway.

Orientation The main road, Rue Mina al-Jadida, runs south to north along the coastline, with the motorway running parallel to it further up the hill. Heading south (left) from the roundabout is the old town centre, Jounieh's prettiest quarter. Here the street is filled with cafés, pubs and some interesting antique stores leading up to and north of the municipality building. Head north of the roundabout on this road and you enter Maameltein district. From the roundabout it's a 10-minute stroll north to the teleferique station, just after St Louis Hospital. The casino is a little further on and accessed from the motorway.

Places in Jounieh

Jounieh is really a place to hang out and spend money in the restaurants, beach clubs and nightclubs, rather than a sightseeing destination. Along **Rue Mina al-Jadida**, some of the beautiful Ottoman-era buildings still survive and the grand old municipality building, with its cream stone façade and blue wooden shutters, is a fine example of architecture of this period. This stretch of road is a see-and-be-seen parade of party goers on summer evenings with cars cruising bumper to bumper and often blasting out music at ear-splitting levels. During the day, even in summer, it's much quieter and makes a pleasant walk.

St George's Grotto Beside the road leading towards the port, St George's grotto provides a reminder of a bygone era. Enclosed within a neatly landscaped area of park is a pond at the foot of an overhanging cliff face with several small shrines dedicated to St George and the Virgin Mary cut into the rocks. This was almost certainly a shrine to Adonis before the Christian period, and the grotto is said to have once been connected via a tunnel with the Greek Catholic monastery of Sarba further up the mountain side, itself built on the site of an ancient acropolis. People still come here to seek cures for their sick children. The landscaped park, the fountains bubbling away in the pond, and the filtered lighting at night are all recent additions, and very typically Lebanese.

The teleferique ① *Behind St Louis Hospital, signposted from Rue Mina al-Jadida, summer Tue-Sun 1000-2200, winter Tue-Sun 1000-1800, 9000 LBP return, children under 10 5000 LBP, price includes the short funicular trip from the Harissa teleferique station to the base of the statue.* Although there is a road leading up to Harissa from Jounieh, the most exciting way to get there is by the teleferique. The brightly coloured gondolas climb steeply from the coast up to the summit, passing indecently close to some of the high-rise apartments en route and providing spectacular views out over the bay. The trip (which is petrifying if you don't have a head for heights) only takes nine minutes, before depositing you in Harissa where you then take a short funicular train to the summit.

At the top is a huge statue of the Virgin Mary, overlooking Jounieh from its mountain perch. Inaugurated in 1908, the 15-tonne bronze statue (now painted white) is known locally as Notre Dame du Liban (our lady of Lebanon). You can join the numerous pilgrims in climbing the spiral staircase around the base of the statue, although you soon realize that for the pilgrims this is a serious religious experience rather than mere sightseeing. There is also a small chapel inside the base of the statue and, nearby, a souvenir shop doing brisk business in religious souvenirs. A short distance to the south of the statue and modernistic cathedral, is the Byzantine-style **St Paul's Basilica**, built between 1947-1962 by a Greek Catholic society of preaching fathers, the Missionaries of St Paul.

Casino du Liban ① *In Maameltein, overlooking the bay of Jounieh from the north, www. cdl.com.lb. The main entrance is via the motorway (heading south the turning is clearly signposted just over 1 km south of the Tabarja exit; heading north, take the Tabarja exit and double back). Open all year round (the gaming rooms from 2000-0400, the slot machine area from 1200-0400). Minimum entry age is 21 and a strict dress code (no denim or sneakers) is enforced.* If ever there was a national symbol of Lebanon's reputation as the 'playground of the Middle East', this is it. The brain-child of Camille Chamoun, president of Lebanon from 1952-1958, and first opened in 1959, the Casino du Liban was an extravagant multimillion dollar project. According to Victor Moussa, the first general manager of the casino, it was conceived as a means of containing the burgeoning gambling industry by bringing it all together in one establishment, while banning gaming activity in the rest of the country. Other commentators have criticized it as a symbol of the grossly iniquitous development policies that Chamoun presided over, favouring the Maronite community at a time when the country was in desperate need of a more balanced approach that would help unite the Christian and Muslim communities and create a sense of common national identity. Be that as it may, the Casino du Liban was built, and soon gained a reputation as one of the most prestigious casinos in the world, attracting the rich and famous from both East and West, and boasting lavish cabarets and musical extravaganzas, a huge theatre and numerous bars and restaurants in addition to the gaming rooms.

Badly damaged and subsequently closed down during the civil war, the casino underwent a massive US$50 million reconstruction and refurbishment programme in the 1990s, and was finally opened to the public once again in 1996. Facilities include 60 gaming tables, a slot machine area with over 300 machines, six restaurants, various bars, a nightclub, and two theatres for the various cabarets that show here.

Byblos (Jbail) → *For listings, see pages 67-70.*

Beautiful little Byblos has an unhurried Mediterranean charm. The medieval town's ramparts and narrow souqs, which ramble down to the tiny fishing harbour, have been immaculately restored and provide a welcome relief from the frenetic pace of life beyond. Bougainvillea spills over stone walls, cobblestones line the streets, and in the harbour tiny pleasure boats bob about in the glistening blue sea. For some it will be a bit twee, with touristy souvenir shops at every turn, but the rich historical heritage here lends Byblos an undeniably evocative atmosphere.

Revered by the Egyptians as the 'land of gods', Byblos shows traces of settlement stretching back through seven millennia and was one of the great city-ports of the ancient Canaanite-Phoenician period. In its heyday, the trade in papyrus between Egypt and Greece was controlled from here and it is from this that Byblos acquired its name (from the Greek for papyrus, 'bublos').

These days the town is full of tourists, not traders, and walking through the winding souqs it's hard to imagine this sleepy place being the centre of anything. A visit to the citadel and its adjacent archaeological site will give you a feel for the vast and glorious history of the town. After scrambling around the ruins, head to the harbour for a drink. This is a place to relax and explore slowly; gazing out at the sparkling blue sea from your shady seat, drink in hand, is the de rigueur activity for any visitor here.

Arriving in Byblos

Getting there All northbound public transport from Beirut's Charles Helou station passes through here. If your bus or service taxi doesn't end in Byblos, you'll be dropped on the motorway just beside the entry road into the town itself. From here, it's a 10-minute stroll to the centre. The same goes for service taxis, buses and minibuses coming from Jounieh, or towns to the north of Byblos. Any transport not terminating in Byblos will not go into the town itself and you will have to walk from the motorway.

The LCC No 6 bus, which begins at Beirut's Cola Junction bus station, is the best option for getting here as it drops you right in the town centre, beside the Federal Bank building.

If you have your own transport there is a large parking area a little to the north of the fishing harbour.

Orientation Byblos is easily explored on foot. From the Federal Bank building, where the LCC No 6 bus terminates, it is a short stroll down the road into the heart of town and the beginning of the medieval ramparts. Old Byblos extends south through the souqs towards the Crusader castle and archaeological site, and west down towards the tiny fishing harbour.

Tourist information There is a small tourist information office ① *T09-540325, daily 0830-1700, in the square at the entrance to the Crusader castle and archaeological site*. You can pick up a selection of Ministry of Tourism brochures, but, other than a friendly welcome, the staff have little else to offer in practical terms.

Background

Earliest settlement The earliest evidence of settlement dates back to around 5000 BC, when a small **neolithic** community lived here in round mud huts and engaged in simple agriculture, animal husbandry and fishing, using implements of stone, wood, bone, and pottery. Obsidian blades found here indicate that some form of trade existed with Anatolia.

During the **Chalcolithic** period (3800-3200 BC), ceramics and copper weapons began to make their appearance, the copper imported from Cyprus and the Caucasus, along with ebony from the Sudan and lapis lazuli from Central Asia. After around 3200 BC, the dwellings show a marked change, the round mud huts being replaced by more sophisticated rectangular buildings, with roofs supported by timber posts and beams. The settlement steadily grew, the houses becoming more densely packed inside an area now enclosed within ramparts.

Foreign influence and trade By the early to mid-third millennium BC, Byblos began to flourish in its role as a great commercial and religious centre. The source of its wealth was timber from the vast cedar forests of Mount Lebanon, which was traded with the Old Kingdom pharaohs of Egypt. By the end of the third millennium BC, trade had reached new heights, with timber, pitch, resin, wool and olive oil being shipped down the coast to Egypt in return for gold, alabaster, papyrus, flax, rope, cereals and pulses. Byblos also traded with Anatolia to the north and Mesopotamia to the east and in effect became a conduit for the passage of goods and ideas between Egypt and these two centres of civilization.

From around 2100 BC Byblos was overrun by waves of **Amorites**, a nomadic Semitic people from the deserts of Arabia. The Amorites settled in Byblos, bringing with them their own influences. Soon, however, trading relations were re-established with the Egyptian pharaohs of the Middle Kingdom and Egyptian influence began to reassert itself, fusing with that of the Amorites and indigenous Giblites (people of Jbail). What emerged is seen by many as the first truly Canaanite culture. Thus the obelisk temple dating from this period was dedicated to Reshef, the Semitic god of war and destruction, while the obelisks themselves were clearly an idea borrowed from Egypt. The temple of Baalat-Gebal, having been partially destroyed by fire, was restored in modified form and worship of Baal-Gebal continued, though with new Semitic influences.

Towards the end of the 18th century BC, the first of several waves of invaders, the **Hyskos** arrived, bringing with them new military techniques in the form of horse-drawn chariots, squadron formations, javelins and lances. They settled in Byblos and overthrew the Middle Kingdom Egyptians, remaining in power for over a century and a half.

However, in 1580 BC the Egyptian pharaohs of the New Kingdom retaliated, driving the Hyskos from Byblos and this time establishing more direct control, with Byblos becoming in effect a vassal state.

By the end of the 13th century BC what is considered to be the forerunner of our own alphabet emerged (the first evidence of it to be found on the sarcophagus of King Ahiram). Although the Ugaritic alphabet came earlier, it still relied on cuneiform imprints on clay tablets, while the script at Byblos was more cursive, making it better suited to writing on papyrus, and so spread more easily through Europe and the West. While Byblos (along with Beirut, Sidon and Tyre) remained faithful allies of the Egyptian pharaohs, other local rulers gave their allegiance instead to the newly emergent **Hittites**, and the famous Tell Amarna tablets of Egypt record the desperate and futile pleas of the kings of Byblos for assistance from the declining pharaohs against the Hittite threat.

Fluctuating fortunes under new masters Ultimately, however, the period of Egyptian domination at Byblos was brought to an end not by the Hittites, but by the arrival of the **Sea Peoples** around 1200 BC. Although the heyday of Phoenician culture is generally identified as coming after this invasion, Byblos itself (perhaps mirroring the fate of Egypt) appears to have fallen into decline, with Tyre to the south and Arwad to the north (ancient Aradus, the island that gave rise to present-day Tartus in Syria) taking the ascendency. The archaeological record shows little in the way of building activity, although Byblos continued as a small centre of trade, most importantly in papyrus between Egypt and Greece, coming first under **Assyrian** and later **neo-Babylonian** (Chaldean) control.

Following the conquest of Babylon by Cyrus the Great in 539 BC, the **Persian** period saw a new flourishing of trading activity and wealth at Byblos. Submitting peacefully to Alexander the Great in 332 BC, it continued to prosper during the **Hellenistic** period, still ruled by its own semi-independent kings.

From the time of Pompey's conquest of the region in 64 BC, the **Roman** period saw Byblos fall into economic decline again, its main source of wealth, the cedar forests of Mount Lebanon having been all but completely exhausted. Nevertheless, it remained an important religious centre based on the cult of Adonis, which survived well into the second century AD, and the Romans undertook an extensive building programme there. During the **Byzantine** period, paganism was gradually replaced by Christianity and Byblos became the seat of a bishopric.

Following the **Arab Muslim** conquest of the seventh century AD, Byblos fell into obscurity and only regained a certain measure of importance during the **Crusader** period. When Byblos was captured by Raymond St Gilles in 1104, a castle was immediately built overlooking the small harbour which gave the town a major strategic significance to the Crusaders. After the death of Raymond in 1105, the town was controlled by the Genoese and benefited from trade with Europe. In 1187 it was captured by Salah ud-Din and colonized with Kurds before being retaken by the Crusaders in 1199 and remaining in their hands until they were finally driven out by Baibars in 1266.

Under **Mamluk** and **Ottoman** rule, although the fortifications left by the Crusaders were repaired in anticipation of their possible return, Byblos returned to relative obscurity, no longer an important centre of trade. The significance of the site was first highlighted by Ernest Renan, who carried out a survey in 1860. Detailed excavations were carried out by Pierre Mentet from 1921-1924 and continued by Maurice Dunand until 1975, when work was interrupted by the civil war.

Places in Byblos

Byblos' medieval town was surrounded by **ramparts**, of which the north section is best preserved, along with parts of the east section. These were first built by the Crusaders in

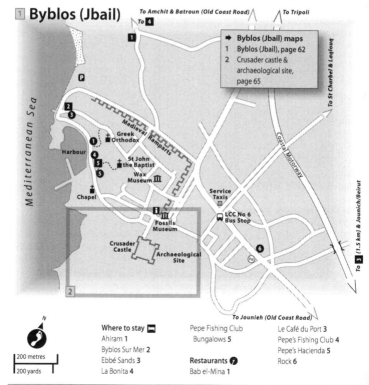

1 **Byblos (Jbail)**

To Amchit & Batroun (Old Coast Road)
To **4**
To Tripoli

➡ Byblos (Jbail) maps
1 Byblos (Jbail), page 62
2 Crusader castle & archaeological site, page 65

Mediterranean Sea

To St Charbel & Laqlouq

Medieval Ramparts

Greek Orthodox

Harbour

St John the Baptist

Wax Museum

Chapel

Fossils Museum

Service Taxis

LCC No 6 Bus Stop

Crusader Castle

Archaeological Site

Coastal Motorway

To **3** (1.5 km) & Jounieh/Beirut

To Jounieh (Old Coast Road)

N

200 metres
200 yards

Where to stay	Pepe Fishing Club	Le Café du Port 3
Ahiram 1	Bungalows 5	Pepe's Fishing Club 4
Byblos Sur Mer 2		Pepe's Hacienda 5
Ebbé Sands 3	Restaurants	Rock 6
La Bonita 4	Bab el-Mina 1	

the early 12th century at the same time as the castle, although they were subsequently repaired during the Mamluk and Ottoman periods and have been further restored in recent years. The cobbled **souqs**, running north–south just outside the east ramparts, and leading north, east and west from the square by the Crusader castle and entrance to the archaeological site, have likewise been carefully restored in recent years and now boast a number of rather naff tourist shops, as well as some more interesting antique shops and small cafés. The overall effect is perhaps a little too neat and contrived, but the beautiful Mamluk and Ottoman period buildings do still have a certain charm.

Fossils museum (Mémoire Du Temps) ① *At the end of the souq near the small square by the entrance to the Crusader castle and archaeological site, www.memoryoftime.com, daily 0900-1800, free.* Opened in 1966, this museum/shop is well worth a visit. The quarries of the nearby towns of Haqel, Hjula and Ennammoura have yielded incredible amounts of well-preserved fossils and the Abi-Saad family have been excavating them for three generations. There are beautifully presented displays of the fossil fish and other organisms found in this region and interesting explanations of their role in helping us understand the evolutionary process. Some are for sale, see Shopping, page 69.

Crusader castle and archaeological site ① *Daily 0800-sunset, 6000 LBP, student 1500 LBP, ask at the ticket office or the tourist information office if you're interested in a guided tour, there are usually multi-lingual guides on hand. There is a small museum with well-displayed finds from the site and documenting the history of Byblos, located within the castle itself (first room on the left after you enter).* Within the site is a somewhat rearranged version of what previously existed. With so many layers of settlement enclosed within such a small area, excavation of the most ancient monuments involved removing later monuments that had been built on top of earlier ones and relocating them. Thus, the small Roman theatre was originally between the northeast entrance of the city and the temple of Reshef/Obelisk temple, but was obstructing excavation of the latter and so was dismantled and moved piece by piece to its present location.

The Crusader castle Built largely from recycled Roman stones and columns, and standing on the site of an earlier Fatimid fortification, the castle consists of a solid central keep or donjon enclosed within defensive walls with towers at each corner and an extra tower in the north wall, defending the original entrance. From the roof of the northwest and southwest towers you can get an excellent overview of the layout of the archaeological site.

You exit the Crusader castle through a small doorway in the base of the northwest tower (follow the steps leading down just beside the main doorway by which you first entered). Turn left to follow the west wall of the castle southwards (note the column drums used to reinforce the lower parts of the castle walls). On your right are the remains of successive stages of the city's ancient ramparts. The three most northerly glacis date from late second to early first millennium BC. Immediately south of these is a glacis of large stone blocks erected during the Hyskos period (1725-1580 BC). The southernmost rampart, clearly identifiable by its regularly spaced square buttresses, dates from the second half of the third millennium BC. To the south of it are indistinct traces of an even earlier rampart dating from the early third millennium BC.

The ramparts to the obelisk temple The ancient ramparts to the east of the Crusader castle (early to mid-third millennium BC) are pierced by a gateway, which was the main entrance to the city. Steps lead up to a narrow passageway between the ramparts and down the other side (though, depending on the season, you may find this route to the Archaemenid Persian fortress overgrown and impassable).

To the south of the gateway are the remains of a **third millennium BC temple** (labelled 'Temple En L, c 2300 BC'), dedicated to an unknown deity. Towards the end of the third millennium it was burnt down, probably during the Amorite invasions. The large depression to the west, now with pine trees growing in part of it, is thought to have been a **sacred pool**, associated with this temple and the contemporary temple of Balaat-Gebal on the opposite side.

To the southeast of the third millennium BC temple is the more interesting **obelisk temple**, now surrounded by a wrought-iron fence and generally kept locked. This temple was built on the ruins of the third millennium BC temple by the Amorites in the early second millennium BC. Standing in the centre of the raised inner sanctuary of the temple is the cube-shaped base of a large obelisk, thought to have been a symbolic representation of Reshef, the god of war and destruction.

Dotted around the surrounding courtyard are numerous smaller obelisks, probably erected by the devout as a means of soliciting the god's favour. Referred to as the masseboth in the scriptures and cursed and doomed to destruction by the prophets, the majority of these obelisks were nevertheless found still in their upright position when the temple was excavated. Numerous votive offerings were also uncovered, consisting of small bronze figurines covered with gold leaf (a collection of these is on display in the National Museum in Beirut).

The king's well From the obelisk temple, a path runs west to the king's well. This consists of a deep crater-like depression at the bottom of which is the base of a well. The sides of the depression are lined with stone and steps lead down to the well itself. Originally this was a spring, which provided the whole of the town's water supply. During the Roman period, a system of earthenware pipes brought water to the town from the surrounding mountains and the spring water was only used for religious purification rituals. However, the rising earth level over the centuries threatened to choke the spring, so a well was constructed, which was still in use as late as 1936. What you see today is the base of the well, the depression having been excavated to the level of the spring to reveal the steps by which it was reached in earlier times.

The great residence To the south of the king's well are traces of a late fourth millennium BC **pre-urban settlement**, while to the west of this are the remains of a large third millennium BC Early Bronze Age settlement, generally referred to as the great residence. This is the best preserved of the settlement compounds dating from this period, consisting of a long central hall with three sets of rooms on either side. The roof of the central hall and those of the side rooms were held up by thick wooden columns, the stone locating bases of which can still be seen (120 of them in all). Some have sought to identify this complex as the palace in which stood the column containing the coffin of Osiris.

A little to the west again, on the edge of the cliffs overlooking the sea, there is a large red-roofed Ottoman period house, the only part of the 19th-20th century village that once covered the whole of the excavation area not to have been cleared away. Dotted around it are the indistinct remains of various neolithic and chalcolithic dwellings (fifth and fourth millennium BC). In the latter, numerous earthenware burial jars were discovered, complete with skeletons inside curled up in foetal positions.

The Roman theatre and royal tombs A rough path leads north from the Ottoman house, passing between an area of Early Bronze Age settlement on the left and a large Amorite quarry on the right, to arrive at the Roman theatre. Built around 218 AD, the theatre is surprisingly small, even taking into account the fact that the four tiers of seating represent only a third of the original number. Note the holes in the first tier, which served to locate poles supporting an awning as protection against the sun. The miniature porticoes decorating the low wall of the stage are unique to this theatre. The square of black basalt pebbles in the centre of the semi-circular pit of the theatre mark the spot where a mosaic of Bacchus, now in the National Museum, once lay.

To the east and north of the theatre are the royal tombs, nine of them in all, dating from the second millennium and consisting of deep shafts dug into the bedrock. Although all but three of them had already been looted by the time they were excavated, many of the sarcophagi remained. The most important, that of king Ahiram, with the earliest known example of alphabetic writing engraved on it (a curse against would-be tomb robbers), is now in the National Museum. Steps lead down into one of the shafts, with a tunnel at

② Crusader castle & archaeological site

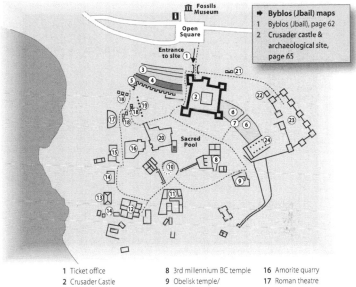

➡ Byblos (Jbail) maps
1 Byblos (Jbail), page 62
2 Crusader castle &
   archaeological site,
   page 65

1 Ticket office
2 Crusader Castle
3 Glacis (late 2nd to
   early 1st millennium BC)
4 Hyskos Glacis
   (1725-1580 BC)
5 Buttressed rampart
   (3rd millennium BC)
6 Ramparts
   (3rd millennium BC)
7 Gateway
8 3rd millennium BC temple
9 Obelisk temple/
   Temple of Reshef
10 King's well
11 Pre-urban settlement
12 Great residence
13 Ottoman building
14 Neolithic and
   Calcolithic dwellings
15 Early Bronze Age
   settlement
16 Amorite quarry
17 Roman theatre
18 Royal tombs
19 Roman colonnade
20 Temple of Baalat-Gebal
21 Roman Nymphaeum
22 Byzantine oil press
23 Achaemenid Persian
   fortress
24 Monumental podium

N

50 metres
50 yards

the bottom giving access to another, where there is a massive stone sarcophagus still in place, that of Yp-shemu-Abi, son of Abi-shemu, a 19th-century BC prince of Byblos.

Along the colonnaded street Up on the hill to the east of the main cluster of royal tombs are the remains of a Roman colonnaded street, with six re-erected columns. These stand on the level of the original mound, giving some idea of the depth to which the surrounding excavations have been carried out. At their south end is the **temple of Baalat-Gebal**. This was the largest and most important of the temples at Byblos. First founded around 3000 BC, it continued to be used right through to the Roman era when it was dedicated to Astarte/Aphrodite (the colonnade street was built by the Romans as an approach to it), undergoing numerous re-buildings and transformations over the intervening millennia. The excavated remains you can see today date from the third millennium BC, when the temple was a focal point for the close relations that developed between Byblos and Egypt. Numerous fragments of alabaster vases given by the pharaohs as offerings were uncovered here, dating from this period. Some of these fragments, inscribed with the names of the Old Kingdom pharaohs of Egypt, including Cheops, the builder of the pyramids (26th century BC), can be seen at the National Museum, and the AUB archaeological museum.

The Roman nymphaeum Returning to the Crusader castle, a path leads under the bridge by which you entered and along the north wall of the castle. By the northeast tower are the remains of a Roman nymphaeum, only its base still standing, but with the remainder laid out on the ground beside it. Beyond this, following the old rail tracks used by the excavators to shift earth and stones, you come to the remains of a **Byzantine oil press**, followed by an **Achaemenid Persian fortress** (late fifth century BC) built against a **monumental podium** (early fifth century BC), which covered part of the ancient ramparts and which was topped by a building.

Church of St John the Baptist (Mar Yuhanna) Built in 1115 in the Romanesque style by the Crusaders, this church underwent several modifications and additions over the subsequent centuries. Perhaps the most striking feature from the outside is the open-sided **baptistry** built onto the side of the church, with its domed top and gracefully decorated arches. Added around 1200, the diverse decoration on the arches of the baptistry, incorporating rosettes, ribbing and zigzags, is clearly Italian in style, reflecting the influence of Genoese who occupied Byblos at this time.

The adjacent entrance is of 18th-century origin, but around the opposite side of the church the entrance is purely Romanesque; note the heavy buttressing along this side, thought to have been added following a severe earthquake in 1170. Inside, the barrel vaulting above the central nave is on an impressive scale. The church suffered serious damage during the British bombardment of 1840 and was only fully restored in 1947, at which point the bell tower was added.

Set within a rectangular garden adjacent to the paved courtyard in which the church stands (on the west side), traces of **mosaic paving**, foundations and a single standing column are all that remain of an earlier Byzantine church. There is grass growing amidst the mosaic, but in places its geometric patterns are discernible.

Across the road is the **Wax Museum** ① *daily 0900-1800, 8000 LBP*, a quirky little place that uses waxwork figures to document the vast history of Byblos. It's a bit cheesy, but some may enjoy it.

A little further down the same street, heading towards the harbour, there is a small Greek Orthodox church, a squat, heavily buttressed, fortress-like structure. The various remains scattered around the church's garden point to its Byzantine origins.

The harbour Walking down to the tiny harbour, it is difficult to imagine that this was the port from which cedar was shipped to the Egyptian pharaohs and that Phoenician merchants carried out extensive trade from here throughout the Mediterranean and beyond. The Crusaders built towers on either side of the narrow harbour mouth, of which the north tower still stands, and controlled entry and exit to and from the port by means of a chain strung between the two. A visit to **Pepe's Fishing Club**, overlooking the harbour, is a must – if not for a meal, then at least for a drink. You can also visit the small private museum here. In summer, some of the fishing boats run short trips out to sea for tourists.

Roman street In the central reservation of the short stretch of dual carriageway running from the old coast road up to the coastal motorway are the remains of the Roman-period main north-south street, or cardo maximus. Around halfway up, traces of the original paving have been excavated, and a series of columns from the colonnade that lined the street re-erected. At the top is a tumbled pile of column sections awaiting re-erection.

North from Beirut listings

For hotel and restaurant price codes and other relevant information, see pages 9-10.

🛏 Where to stay

Byblos (Jbail) *p59, map p62*
As Byblos is an easy day trip from Beirut, it doesn't have much in the way of accommodation options. There's no proper budget accommodation in town, but there's a campground in the nearby town of Amchit. Outside of the high season, Byblos' hotels usually offer good discounts.
$$$$ Eddé Sands, just south of Byblos town, T09 546085, www.eddesands. com. This chic resort exudes a relaxed yet luxurious vibe and is the perfect beach getaway on this strip of the coast. The stone-walled beachfront bungalows, with their bamboo-shaded roof terraces and piles of wicker furniture, are a lesson in simple elegance. It's the sort of place where it's de rigueur to have sand between your toes while sipping your cocktail overlooking the setting sun. The entire complex is massive, with tastefully manicured lawns, a spa, several restaurants and bars, swimming pools and, obviously, a beach. There's also the option of cheaper beach cabanas and rooms within the adjacent Sands Hotel. Breakfast included.
$$$ Ahiram, overlooking the sea a little way to the north of the port and Old Town, T09-540440, www.ahiramhotel. com. In a quiet residential location, this hotel has access to the public beach below. Although nothing special, the rooms here are spacious, come with a/c, satellite TV and fridge, and have decent bathrooms. Some also have balconies with sea views. There are great discounts for long stays. Breakfast included, bar, restaurant.
$$$ Byblos Sur Mer, Byblos Port, T09-548000, www.byblossurmer.com. The top hotel in Byblos' old town, Byblos Sur Mer is ideally located overlooking the sea right by the old port. Rooms come with all the modern comforts you'd expect, are full of classical design features and have luxurious bathrooms. Many sport supreme sea views. It's a lovely and elegant place to stay. Restaurants, bar, parking, Wi-Fi.
$$ La Bonita, 2nd right-hand intersection after passing the Ahiram Hotel, T09-543666,

Pepe Abed and the Byblos Fishing Club

Entertainment maestro, head raconteur, enthusiastic amateur archaeologist, friend of the famous and beautiful people; Pepe Abed led a full and adventurous life and became a local legend.

Born of mixed Lebanese and Mexican parentage, Pepe grew up in Mexico and travelled extensively before coming to Lebanon and establishing his restaurant on the harbour at Byblos. With his charm and charisma, as well as his natural talent for throwing a damn good party, Pepe's Fishing Club soon became a vital stop for the rich and famous who, in the party heydays of the 1960s, arrived in their droves. Marlon Brando, Sophia Loren, Brigitte Bardot, David Niven, David Rockefeller, Mick Jagger, Carlos Menem, Vaklav Havel and countless others have all graced the Fishing Club with their presence, as a collage of fading photographs documents.

Not content to just be a party-starter, Pepe was also a keen diver and collector of archaeological artefacts, and he set about establishing a small museum to display his collection. Dedicated under the auspices of UNESCO, this remarkable collection spans the Phoenician, Persian, Greek and Roman periods and includes statues, jewellery, amphorae, anchors, friezes and capitals; all retrieved by Pepe from the sea around Byblos over the years. It also includes various Mayan artefacts brought back from Mexico.

Pepe may no longer be around, but his legend prevails. At the helm these days are Pepe's son Roger and his grandson Pepe Junior. They keep Pepe's spirit alive and are often on hand to greet customers personally. Pepe's party might be over, but the Fishing Club is still going strong after 60 years.

www.labonita-resort.com. This slightly run-down hotel has huge, sparsely furnished studios that include a kitchenette (fridge, stove, sink), simple bathroom, a/c and satellite TV. More expensive rooms come with a separate lounge area as well. It's all a bit devoid of personality, but is reasonably clean and a good option for those who want to self-cater.

$$ Pepe's Fishing Club Bungalows, behind Pepe's Fishing Club restaurant, T09-540213. These delightful, secluded bungalows on the hill behind the port are unfortunately often booked up for the entire summer by long-stays. If you do manage to bag one, they're a cute and quirky option. All include a kitchenette and bathroom and some have their own tiny private gardens.

$ Camping Les Colombes, Amchit, on the coast 2 km to the north of Byblos, on the motorway once past Byblos, turn right at MacDonald's and follow the signs from there, if coming by bus ask to get off at Amchit's motorway overpass, cross and follow signs from there, T09-622401, www.campinglescolombes.com. Lebanon's first campsite (opened in 1965) and the only real budget place on the coast between Beirut and Tripoli. It's within easy walking distance of Byblos and also useful as a base for trips up the Adonis Valley and to surrounding areas. There's a range of accommodation here, from comfortable chalets with all mod cons and their own private bathrooms, to the very cramped and rather claustrophobic 'tungalows' (permanent tent-structures). You can also pitch your own tent or park up your camper-van here. The campground has shared bathrooms and 2 shared kitchens and direct access onto the rocky beach below (there's no shop, restaurant or other services offered, so you have to be self-sufficient).

Restaurants

Jounieh p57

There are restaurants and snack places lining the road through Kaslik, the old coast road through Jounieh, and the motorway.
$$$ Chez Sami, Rue Mina al-Jadida, Maameltein, T09-910520. This stylish Levantine restaurant is set in a carefully restored Ottoman building complete with its own outdoor seafront deck. It's the perfect place to try a variety of Lebanese meze that it's justly famous for. The fish, though pricey, is also superb. A real treat of a restaurant. Reservation essential.
$$ Don Carlos, Rue Mina al-Jadida, Maameltein. It may look a little down-at-heel from the outside, but this little restaurant does some great latin-inspired dishes and is an atmospheric place to hang out.
$$ Piscine, Rue Mina al-Jadida, old Jounieh. Another place with a seafront terrace, Piscine has a decent (if a bit generic) menu of grills and seafood and is a pleasant stop for lunch.
$ Toni, Rue Mina al-Jadida, old Jounieh. A decent snack-style café with pavement seating outside that has good sandwiches for 3000-7000 LBP and crêpes for 6000 LBP. The ice cream sundaes are bliss on a hot day and there's a wide and rather unusual range of juices.

Byblos (Jbail) p59, map p62

If you want to eat on the cheap, there are several decent snack bars and takeaways along the old coast road as it passes through town. The best falafel and *shawarma* can be found at the **Rock**, a brightly lit and spotlessly clean place that also does kebabs.
$$$ Bab el-Mina, beside harbour, T09-540475. Daily 1200-late. As at their more famous neighbour's next door (Pepe's Fishing Club), Bab el-Mina's terrace is a nice spot to sit back with a drink and take in the views. Unsurprisingly, the menu is strong on seafood and they've got a decently priced set menu. A good choice if Pepe's is full.

$$$ Pepe's Fishing Club, beside harbour, T09-540213. Daily 1200-late. It wouldn't be a full Byblos experience if you missed a meal at Pepe's. This place has been going strong for 60 years now and is still the place to go. Pepe's gives a glimpse of the good old days, when the rich and famous came here. A meal here won't break the bank. Seafood is the speciality, and you can choose your fish, caught fresh that day, straight from the display. The set menu is excellent value at US$22, including a meze, a main course of fish or grill, fruit for dessert and coffee. After your meal ask to see Pepe's museum, see page 68. Highly recommended.
$$ Le Café du Port, opposite Byblos Sur Mer Hotel, T09-547447. Daily 1100-late. The garden terrace here is a relaxing place to while away a couple of hours over some good meze with friends. A full seafood meal will cost US$20 upward.
$$ Pepe's Hacienda, just before the harbour. 1700-late. A lovely shady garden that has a simple menu of pasta and pizza. If you're not hungry it's a nice place for a wine or a beer.

Festivals

Byblos (Jbail) p59, map p62
Jul Byblos Festival, www.byblosfestival. org. This month-long celebration of music attracts international big names as well as local musicians. A series of evening concerts are held throughout July and vary from rock and pop to classical Arabic.

Shopping

Byblos (Jbail) p59, map p62
There are plenty of tourist shops selling souvenirs, jewellery and handicrafts in the restored Ottoman souqs of the old town, and around the small square by the entrance to the Crusader castle and archaeological site.
Mémoire Du Temps, at the end of the souq near the small square by the entrance to the

Crusader castle and archaeological site, www. memoryoftime.com. Daily 0900-1800. For a more unusual gift, this shop/museum sells rocks bearing imprints of fossil fish in a range of prices. All fossils come with a certificate of authenticity. If you are interested in these you might also want to consider visiting the small village of Haqel, 17 km away in the mountains to the east of Byblos, where most of these fossils are found and where there are several more shops selling them.

🏃 What to do

Byblos (Jbail) *p59, map p62*
To the south of the fishing harbour a path leads to a small bay at the foot of the cliffs below the excavated archaeological site, where there is an excellent sand beach, free and open to the public.

Just to the north of the fishing harbour (below the Ahiram Hotel) there is a short stretch of public beach with a couple of snack bars. The beach here is shingle, but it is reasonably clean. Note that the beach shelves quite steeply into the water, so it's not really suitable for children.

Heading south out of Byblos towards Jounieh, and reached by turnings off the old coast road and motorway, there is a series of private beach clubs of which the massive **Eddé Sands** (day access with full use of resort facilities, weekends 30,000 LBP, weekdays 25,000 LBP, under 10-years 10,000), is the nicest option.

⊖ Transport

Jounieh *p57*
To **Beirut** the LCC No 6 bus, trundles down the northern section of Rue Mina al-Jadida (before turning up the hill, to join the motorway, at the roundabout next to KFC) on its way from Byblos to Cola Junction bus station (1 hr, flat fare 1500 LBP). One comes along about every 15 mins. It's not the fastest way back to Beirut due to the roundabout route it takes once inside the

city. Let the driver know if you want to get off before Cola Junction. The bus route takes you past Dora Junction and the Beirut National Museum which, depending where you're staying, is usually a more convenient stop to get off at. Ask the bus driver for 'mat-haf' (museum).

Most other buses, service taxis and minibuses heading to Beirut from the north go via the motorway and you can hail them down at any point along it (30 mins-1 hr depending on traffic, 2000 LBP). They also usually go via Dora Junction and the Museum.

Private taxis in Jounieh usually hang out by the teleferique.

Byblos (Jbail) *p59, map p62*
Service taxis congregate in the centre of town, on the old coast road close to the main entrance to the souqs and leaving when full. Service taxis to **Beirut** (via Jounieh) finish at Dora Junction bus stand (45 mins, 3000 LBP).

Buses and minibuses heading for **Beirut** from Tripoli and other points to the north can be hailed from the motorway. The **Connex** bus from Tripoli goes past regularly and can drop you at either Dora Junction or at Charles Helou bus station. It also sometimes goes via the Beirut National Museum – ask the driver for 'mat-haf' (45 mins depending on traffic, 3000 LBP).

The **LCC No 6** bus to Beirut's Cola Junction bus station leaves roughly every 15 mins from outside the Federal Bank Building on the old coast road (1½ hrs, 1500 LBP). It's route through Beirut also usually takes you past the National Museum.

🛈 Directory

Jounieh *p57*
Medical services Pharmacy Lara, is a well-stocked pharmacy on Rue Mina al-Jadida next to the BLC Bank. **St Louis Hospital**, T09-912970, is a private hospital with good facilities, opposite the teleferique station.

The Metn

Directly east of Beirut, the mountains of the Metn rise steeply from the coastal plain. A number of summer resorts have grown up in these mountains – places where Beirutis can come to escape the heat and humidity of the city. The most popular are Beit Meri and Broummana, which can both be visited as a short round trip from Beirut, returning via the town of Bikfaya on the alternative route between Beirut and Zahle. While the views may be impressive and the summer climate appealing, the popularity of this region and its proximity to Beirut have also in a sense been its undoing, with an often ugly sprawl of development spreading up the mountains along the roads leading out of Beirut.

Beit Meri and Broummana → For listings, see pages 76-79.

At an altitude of 770-800 m above sea level, both Beit Meri and Broummana are refreshingly cool in summer and offer spectacular views out over Beirut and the Mediterranean. Beit Meri, where the archaeological site of Deir el-Qalaa is located, has grown to a considerable size in recent years, with numerous private villas and apartments belonging to rich Beirutis spread across the hillside. There are a couple of hotels here, and on the road between Beit Meri and Broummana, but it is Broummana itself that is the prime summer resort.

Broummana is spread out for several kilometres along the main road, with another road running parallel to the southeast. There is nothing of special interest as such here, this being more a place to come and enjoy the views and lively atmosphere in summer, dine out in style and indulge in a bit of nightlife.

Arriving in Beit Meri and Broummana

If you're coming by public transport, LCC bus No 7 leaves about every 20 minutes from near the National Museum in Beirut and travels through Beit Meri, Broummana and onto Bikfaya.

If you're driving from Beirut it can be a little tricky to navigate your way out of the city to pick up the road to Beit Meri. Head southeast from Downtown on Rue de Damas. Turn left at the National Museum junction and then after around 500 m turn right at the large intersection and flyover to join the broad dual carriageway of Ave Elias Hrawi (signposted for Chtaura). Follow signs for Sin el-Fil (this involves looping underneath Ave Elias Hrawi by the glass Cellis building), and then for Mkalles. Arriving at a large roundabout ('Place Sin el-Fil'), turn right. At the next roundabout ('Place Mkalles'), go straight across, this being the start of the road up to Beit Meri and Broummana (signposted 'Route de Baabdat').

The road climbs steeply into the mountains through a more or less continuous sprawl of suburbs. Some 2 km from the Mkalles roundabout the road forks; left is signposted for Beit Meri, though in fact both branches join up again before Beit Meri. Going by either route, a little over 9 km from the Mkalles roundabout, soon after a sign announcing the start of Beit Meri, you can either follow the road sharply round to the left to continue on to Broummana, or bear off to the right to visit Deir el-Qalaa (see below; signposted 'Ruines de Beit-Mery' on a Ministry of Tourism signboard). Following the road sharply round to the left, after just over 1 km bear left at a roundabout with a column in the centre. A little under 2 km further on, you have the option of forking left (signposted 'Centre Ville') by the massive new **Grand Hills** resort, or else carrying straight on. Both roads take you through Broummana before joining up again at the western end of town; the left fork is the more interesting route through town and gives the best views. ▸▸ See Transport, page 78.

Deir el-Qalaa
① Daily sunrise-sunset, free. To reach the site, bear right at the junction soon after the start of Beit Meri (coming from Beirut; see route description, above), and then bear right again at a mini roundabout 400 m further on. After a further 400 m or so, a track off to the left (with a large Ministry of Tourism sign beside it) leads up to the site.

Deir el-Qalaa consists of a 17th-century Maronite monastery standing on the ruins of a Roman temple, with further Roman and Byzantine ruins nearby. The most interesting sight here is the beautiful piece of mosaic flooring hidden away amid the tumble of weeds in the Roman/Byzantine ruin area. If you are staying in Beit Meri or nearby Broummana, or have come here for the day to escape the city heat below, this site is well worth visiting.

Inscriptions discovered here by Julius Löytved (the vice-consul of Denmark during the late 19th century and a keen amateur archaeologist) have identified the Roman temple

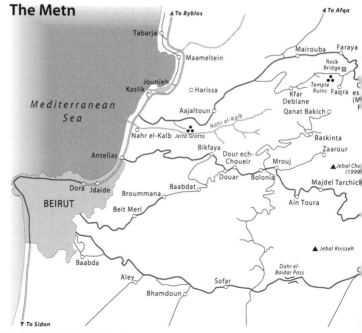

as being dedicated to *Baal Marcod* (the 'Lord of Dances'), and there is evidence to suggest that this was built on the site of an earlier Phoenician temple.

The **Maronite monastery**, built of stones from the Roman temple, was heavily damaged during the civil war, but since then has been extensively restored. A number of hefty columns can be seen, including one built into the wall of the monastery, and also a large square platform built of massive stone blocks, possibly the base of the *cella* of the Roman temple. Nearby there are the remains of other smaller temples, including one dedicated to the goddess Juno, dating from the reign of Trajan (AD 98-117).

Heading back down the road, on both sides, there is an extensive area of **Roman and Byzantine** ruins mostly consisting of fallen columns and capitals amidst overgrown scrub and unfortunately strewn with rubbish. Although these ruins may look unsubstantial at first, on the right-hand side of the road is a very impressive area of **mosaic flooring** that was part of a sixth-century Byzantine church and also the remains of a baths complex. Both are behind the first house you come to.

A driving route through the Metn to Zahle
→ *For listings, see pages 76-79.*

As well as offering a much quieter and more scenic route to Zahle compared with the main Beirut–Damascus highway, this road gives you excellent views of Jebel Sannine. Note that beyond Mrouj, the road is blocked by snow during the winter; if you wish to attempt it in early spring or late autumn, check first that it is open. A lengthy diversion off this route brings you to the small ski resort of **Qanat Bakich**, from where you can also continue on to **Faqra**. En route to Qanat Bakich you pass through the village of **Baskinta**, from where a narrow mountain road loops around the lower slopes of Jebel Sannine to rejoin the Bikfaya–Zahle road between Majdel Tarchich and Zahle.

Beirut to Bikfaya
From Beirut, join the coastal motorway heading north and take the Antelias exit. The road climbs steadily through a more or less continuous built-up sprawl to arrive at Bikfaya (14 km from the motorway exit), the start of which is marked by a roundabout with a large modernistic monument in the centre. Bearing sharp right here (signposted to Baabdat and Broummana, among others) puts you on the road to **Broummana** and Beit Meri (see page 71). Continuing straight on into the centre of town, bear right after 600 m to pick up the road for **Dhour ech-Choueir** (signposted) and **Zahle** (going straight leads you into a confusing though very scenic maze of tiny mountain roads).

You can continue northeast from Broummana along a picturesque road leading to Bikfaya. After passing through the village of Baabdat, there is a viewpoint offering excellent views of Jebel Knisseh to the right (east). Soon after, go straight across a roundabout (right for Douar) and then through a couple more villages to arrive at a roundabout at the eastern end of **Bikfaya**, 11 km from Broummana. Turn sharp left here to head back down to Beirut, joining the coastal motorway at Antelias.

Bikfaya

Bikfaya has a certain air of prosperity about it. This is the home town of the Gemayel family; Pierre Gemayel, founder of the Phalange party in 1936; Bashir Gemayel, the leader of the Phalange militia and Lebanese president-elect for less than a month before his murder in 1982; and Amin Gemayel, Lebanese president from 1982-1988. Their presence is strongly stamped on the town, most notably in the family's 'Presidence', a beautiful Ottoman period mansion signposted off to the left (north) of the main road (though strictly off-limits unless you have some pretty good connections). Bikfaya suffered heavily during 1987 when fighting broke out between the Phalange and various other Christian militias for control of the area. However, the wealth and influence of the Gemayel family ensured that it was rapidly rebuilt. During August of each year a **flower festival** is held here. There are several restaurants and a number of hotels, but otherwise the town has little to offer of special interest. During summer, service taxis run from Dora Junction in Beirut to Bikfaya and there are minibuses from here as well. Services are much less frequent in winter.

Bikfaya to Baskinta and Qanat Bakich

Heading out of Bikfaya on the road towards Dhour ech-Choueir, you pass first through the village of **Douar**, where the damage caused by the internecine fighting between Christian militias in 1987 can still be seen.

Continue straight through the village, passing a right turn leading towards Broummana and Beit Meri, to arrive in **Dhour ech-Choueir**, 5 km from Bikfaya. Travelling in this direction, the main road bypasses the centre of the village; turn left to reach the centre, where there is the imposing Maronite St Mary's church. Continuing along the main road, you pass through a beautiful area of pine forest known as **Bois de Boulogne** (marked on most maps as **Bolonia**), arriving after 7 km at a crossroads and checkpoint. To make the diversion to **Baskinta** and **Qanat Bakich**, turn left at the crossroads.

Heading towards Qanat Bakich, the road descends to the village of **Bteghrine** (follow signs for Baskinta and Qanat Bakich). You may have to ask directions through the village as the route through it is rather confusing. From here the road winds its way steeply down into the deep Wadi el-Jamajin and up the other side to arrive in **Baskinta** (15 km from the crossroads). Turn sharp left in the village (signposted in Arabic only, so ask directions), and then bear right at a fork 1 km further on (signposted to Qanat Bakich, and also to Faqra and Faraya). The road climbs steadily for a further 7 km to arrive in **Qanat Bakich**.

Baskinta

The picturesque town of Baskinta, with its abundance of traditional red-roofed buildings so typical of this region, is interesting for its many literary connections. This was the home town of the poet Mikhail Neameh who, along with Khalil Gibran, was a founding member of the New York literary society The Pen League, and his tomb and family's summer house can be seen in the village. These are just two sites that form part of the larger **Baskinta Literary Trail** (BLT); a 24-km walking route that begins here.

The BLT passes 22 literary landmarks in the countryside around Baskinta, showcasing this area's importance in Lebanon's artistic heritage. As well as Mikhail Neaimeh, this town and the surrounding area has also played host to, among others, the poet and journalist Abdullah Ghanem and the artist Georges Aroyan. Nearby in Ain el Qabou, which the BLT passes through, is the summer home of Amin Maalouf, one of Lebanon's most internationally famous writers, who currently resides in France.

There is an excellent accommodation option within Baskinta itself, making it a great place to spend a couple of days walking in the surrounding countryside and enjoying the quiet pace of life.

Qanat Bakich ski resort
ⓘ *Mon-Fri 0800-1530, Sat-Sun/public holidays 0800-1600, US$10 weekdays, US$18 weekends.* First established in 1967 by the Karam family who built the first ski lift here, Qanat Bakich suffered considerable damage during the civil war and had to be completely redeveloped afterwards. This resort, popular in the early 1970s for its good snow and interesting slopes, is Lebanon's smallest and its non-crowded slopes are a definite bonus. It's an excellent choice for less experienced skiers, with four out of their five slopes suitable for beginners. Ski and snowboard equipment can be hired from the **Snowland Hotel** (the resort's one accommodation option) or from one of the rental shops nearby. Full equipment hire generally costs US$5-12. Those wanting to stay overnight are not limited to the Snowland, as the accommodation at nearby Faraya village is only a 10-minute drive away.

Qanat Bakich to Faqra
From the Snowland Hotel, bear right for the ski lift; if you bear left it is a further 4 km on to the private **Faqra Ski Club** (see page 81). On a clear day, you can see spectacular views down the Wadi Daraiya and Nahr el-Kalb Valley to the Mediterranean. When arriving in Faqra Ski Club you'll see a barrier across the road, but the attendant seems happy to let people through. You can then continue on to Faraya/Mzaar and/or head back down to the coast via Aajaltoun.

Baskinta to Zahle
To carry on to Zahle you can either head back to the crossroads and checkpoint or continue straight using the following directions.

From the crossroads and checkpoint, 1 km further on you arrive at a roundabout and church in the centre of **Mrouj**. Turn right here for Zahle (or straight on – keeping the church to your left – to reach the private, members-only skiing club of **Zaarour**, 7 km away). Taking the Zahle road, after 5 km you pass through **Ain Toura**, a small, rather ugly village consisting mostly of new concrete buildings. The road then begins to climb steeply into the beautiful and rugged limestone mountains of Jebel ech-Chaoukat/Jebel Knisseh. At **Majdel Tarchich** (9 km from Mrouj) there are a couple of snack places. The road continues to climb through a surreal landscape of weathered limestone rock before reaching the crest of the mountains, from where there are stunning views down into the Bekaa Valley, with the Anti-Lebanon Mountains beyond. From here the road descends steadily down to Zahle, 31 km from Mrouj.

Alternatively, if you continue straight on through the village of Baskinta (not taking the sharp left to head up to Qanat Bakich), you can rejoin the Bikfaya–Zahle road roughly halfway between Majdel Tarchich and Zahle. This narrow and extremely beautiful mountain road works its way around the head of the green and wooded

Jamajin Valley, with the bare, imposing southwest slopes of Jebel Sannine rising majestically above.

After around 8 km you pass through the village of **Sannine**, where there are several restaurants all with stunning views down the valley. From here, the road climbs up over the lower slopes of Jebel Sannine, passing a couple of small, high-altitude lakes before descending and arriving at the Bikfaya–Zahle road (19 km from Baskinta). Turning left, it is around 11 km down to Zahle, or turning right, around 20 km to Mrouj.

The Metn listings

For hotel and restaurant price codes and other relevant information, see pages 9-10.

◉ Where to stay

Beit Meri and Broummana *p71*
Not a place for budget travellers, during summer Beit Meri and Broummana attract their fair share of Gulf and local tourists who retreat here for a cool respite from the coast. Many rent apartments for the entire summer and the hotels here tend to be on the expensive side, so if you're in that price bracket and not a city person, both Beit Meri and Broummana are good alternatives to staying in Beirut.

Price categories quoted here are for the high season, when advance booking is recommended. During the low season most hotels offer substantial discounts.

Traditionally, the high season lasts from the beginning of May or Jun through to the end of Nov or Dec, though in practice it is much shorter these days, really only lasting from mid-Jul through to mid-Sep. All the hotels listed below stay open year round.

$$$$ Al Bustan, Beit Meri (signposted from all directions), T04-972980. A wonderful alternative to the international chain hotels of Beirut, the Al Bustan is a family-owned, independent hotel that sits high and mighty over the village of Beit Meri. The surrounding views of the countryside are superb, and the hotel supports the arts (it hosts an annual festival and has its own art collection on display throughout the hotel). Rooms are definitely comfortable but it's still a tad expensive for what you get. Swimming pool, several bars and restaurants, excellent conference facilities, free airport pickup, Wi-Fi, breakfast included.

$$$$ Grand Hills, Rue Al Charkiah, Broummana, T04-868888, www.grandhillsvillage.com. If you're after all-encompassing resort swish, Grand Hills has it in spades. This massive complex is a luxurious hideaway from the rest of the world with 3 swimming pools, its own spa, gym, multiple restaurants and bars, a shopping arcade and huge gardens. The rooms here have all the mod cons you'd expect and have been decorated according to 'theme'. The result, on the whole, is that they are elegant and individually quirky, but it must be said that some of the room 'themes' do verge on the tacky.

$$$ Garden, Broummana centre, T04-960579, www.gardenhotellb.com. This friendly family hotel has decent-sized rooms (a/c, satellite TV) that all come with balcony, and there's a swimming pool and restaurant too. Outside of peak season the discounts you can get are brilliant value.

$$$ Kanaan, Broummana centre, T04-960084. A good value and decent place right across the road from Broummana high school. Grab a room with a balcony if you can. Outside of peak season room rates are slashed heavily.

$$$ Le Crillon, Broummana centre, T04-865555, www.lecrillon.com. Welcoming and family-run, the rooms here (a/c, satellite TV, minibar and balcony) are decent-sized, clean and bright, though they are more business-style rather than a holiday hotel. Restaurant, bar, swimming pool, gym, Wi-Fi.

$$$ Printania Palace, Rue Chahine Achkar, Broummana, T04-862000, www.printania.com. The tasteful, though slightly bland, rooms (a/c, satellite TV, balcony and minibar) here are set back from the road and surrounded by gardens, making this a quiet retreat. With resort-like facilities (restaurants, swimming pool, large grounds with children's play area), it's quite good value compared with some of the other hotels in the area, though asking an extra US$18 for breakfast is a bit steep.

$$ Pax, Broummana centre, T04-960027. A welcoming place with a peculiar pink colour scheme that thankfully doesn't follow you into the rooms. The rooms could do with a refurb and the bathrooms are a tad on the small side, but they're clean and all come with a/c, satellite TV, fridge and balcony. The large sun terrace on the roof with its hilarious lurid green fake-grass carpet is an added bonus.

Bikfaya to Baskinta and Qanat Bakich *p74*
$$ Grand Hotel Bois de Boulogne, on the right immediately before the check-post and crossroads, Bois de Boulogne, T04-295100, www.hotelboisdeboulogneliban.com. This grand old dame of a hotel is a lovely old-fashioned place that evokes an atmosphere of yesteryear. Pleasant rooms (a/c, satellite TV, Wi-Fi and balcony) are clean and decently sized and there are also larger bungalows nestled between the leafy trees in the large garden out back.

Baskinta *p74*
$$ Khoury Hanna Guesthouse, T04-250084. This delightful family guesthouse is set in one of Baskinta's traditional stone-walled and red-tiled houses, with much of its original interior features preserved. The simple and super-clean rooms here, along with the delicious food and the welcoming

hosts, make it a great place to stop for the night if you're exploring the area.

Qanat Bakich ski resort *p75*
$$ Snowland, T03-340300 (or Beirut T01-870077), www.snowland.com.lb. Qanat Bakich's only hotel, the Snowland is right on the slopes and has good-value rooms that are simple but comfortable (satellite TV, heater, some with balcony) and helpful staff. There are great facilities here for the price, with a heated indoor swimming pool, restaurant serving decently priced meals and all the amenities you need for a ski holiday: ski hire, ski school, a first-aid team based at the hotel on weekends and ski lifts right outside. It's an excellent family choice.

⑦ Restaurants

Beit Meri and Broummana *p71*
These summer retreats are all about the food. Boasting some excellent fine dining options, places here tend to be on the pricey side and are patronized by a 'see-and-be-seen' crowd. If you're on a budget there's a few less expensive options strung out on Broummana's main road, but nothing of particular note. There are also 2 excellent supermarkets to stock up on essentials. Both **Bechara** and **Ara** supermarket are on the main road, next door to each other.

$$$ Burj al-Hamam, around 1 km out of Broummana, heading towards Baabdat and Bikfaya (signposted off to the right of the road), T04-960058. Daily 1200-late. This huge and upmarket restaurant provides something of a spectacle in summer, when the seriously rich come here in their droves to dine. All your favourite meze and grills feature on the menu, which focuses on finely done Lebanese staples. Dress smart and arrive in a flash car or you may not be made to feel overly welcome.

$$$ Il Giadino, Al Bustan hotel, Beit Meri. This long-standing Italian restaurant is your best bet in town if you're feeling like a plate of pasta. The tasty dishes here may be expensive but they're well executed and definitely worth it.

$$$ Le Gargotier, Broummana centre, T04-960562. Tue-Sun 1200-1500, 1900-2400. First established in 1971, this cosy traditional French restaurant is an intimate and stylish dining option that's perfect for a romantic dinner for 2.

$$$ Mounir, off main road between Beit Meri and Broummana (coming from Broummana, just after you pass the **Bellevue Palace Hotel**, a signposted fork off to the right leads down steeply to the restaurant), T04-873900. Daily 1200-late. The foodie's choice, Mounir is famous for its perfectly executed Levantine cuisine. A wonderful place for a late, long and lazy lunch, this large and very classy upmarket Lebanese restaurant has extensive gardens and a terrace. If you're travelling with kids, they'll be kept happy with a children's play area on site. It's pricey, but the food really is excellent.

$$ Kings, Broummana centre. Popular American-diner style place with comfy booth-type seating. There's a large menu of burgers and other fast-food style favourites.

$ Café Kanaan, Broummana centre. The friendly atmosphere here makes it a continually popular spot. This place is excellent value, with a delicious menu of pizzas, burgers and crêpes all under 10,000 LBP. It hovers undecidedly between a bar and a café/restaurant, so it's as good for a lunchtime snack on the terrace as it is for a few beers in the evening.

☻ Entertainment

Beit Meri and Broummana *p71*
As a popular summer getaway from Beirut, Broummana has plenty of bars to service the party crowd. Late in the evening it can get pretty hectic and crowded.
Cheers, Broummana centre. A no-nonsense bar set inside a lovely vaulted room that can get packed out on Fri and Sat nights in the

height of summer. The service is great and the crowd is friendly, but don't come here for a quiet drink because this place does loud like it's going out of fashion.
Oaks Pub, Broummana centre. A lovely relaxed place to come for a few drinks. Slightly more refined than the other choices in town.
Taboo Pub, Broummana centre. Although it was pumping out some pretty tacky music when we visited, it's forgiven for its quick, friendly service and good-time crowd.

✦ Festivals

Beit Meri and Broummana *p71*
Feb-Mar Al Bustan Festival, www. albustanfestival.com. Lebanon's only major winter festival is a feast of classical music, theatre and dance. Over 30 performances are staged over a 5-week period with the main venue being at the Al Bustan Hotel.

♦ What to do

Baskinta *p74*
As one of the villages along the Lebanon Mountain Trail (and also having its own literary-based hiking trail) Baskinta is a great base for hiking and trekking in the region. Some good, local hiking guides are:
Carlos Hobeika, T03-580901.
Carole Akl, T03-825064.
George Hobeika, T03-451113.

⊖ Transport

Beit Meri and Broummana *p71*
Both the red and white **LCC No 7** bus and the blue and white **OFTC No 17** bus wind their way up and down the main roads of Beit Meri and Broummana throughout the day. The OFTC bus heads as far as **Bikfaya**, while the LCC bus doubles back a couple of kilometres short of Bikfaya. You can flag them down anywhere along the route. The LCC bus has the most frequent services, with a bus usually every 20 mins

or so throughout the day. Heading back to **Beirut** (45 mins), both buses terminate just to the southeast of the National Museum. Journeys on this route are a flat fee of 1000 LBP.

If you get stuck with no transport back to Beirut the **Achkar taxi office** (T04-961041) is on Broummana's main road.

Directory

Beit Meri and Broummana *p71*
Laundry Right beside Café Kanaan, Clean Xpress has fast and efficient service.
Medical services Just opposite Bank Med, **Pharmacy Joe** is well stocked and has English-speaking staff.

Mount Lebanon Skiing

The Mount Lebanon region is a winter-sports enthusiast's dream. The old Lebanese tourism slogan 'ski in the morning, swim in the afternoon' may be pushing things a bit but you can definitely launch yourself onto the slopes during the day and still get back to Beirut in time for a late dinner.

During the season the roads up into the mountains can be bumper-to-bumper traffic as keen skiers and snowboarders head to the slopes. When the snow disappears most of the resorts press the snooze button and revert back to charmingly sleepy alpine hamlets.

Faraya village and Mzaar Resort → *For listings, see pages 85-88.*

During the winter the area around Faraya and Mzaar comes to life, with many people renting chalets and apartments for the whole season, and many more make the trip up from Beirut at the weekends. Without the snow, however, there is not very much to do, other than visit the dramatic ruins at Faqra. But it is a wonderfully serene and peaceful place to be during summer, and a welcome respite from the humidity of the coast. There are several hotels in and around Faraya, and directly below the Mzaar ski-lift centres in an area known as Ouyoun es-Simaan.

Arriving in Faraya and Mzaar
Orientation The village of Faraya lies around 6 km below the actual ski resort, which is known as Mzaar or Ouyoun es-Simaan. The ski lifts to the slopes are about 1 km further on up the road. Turning left at the roundabout in the centre of Faraya, the road climbs steadily, before arriving at a checkpoint and junction after a little under 5 km. Turning right at this junction takes you past the rock bridge, the turning for Faqra Ski Club, and the temple ruins of Faqra (see 'Faqra' below), while continuing straight on, you arrive soon after in Ouyoun es-Simaan and then, just above, the main Mzaar ski lift, known as Jonction. There is a second ski lift (called Wardeh) a further 2 km up the road.

Skiing at Mzaar
ⓘ *Mon-Fri 0800-1530, Sat-Sun/public holidays 0800-1600, weekdays US$27, under 16-years US$20, weekends US$40, under 16-years US$30, weekdays half-day pass (after 1200), US$17, weekends half-day pass US$23.*
This is Lebanon's most popular resort; it teems with people on the weekends, so plan to come on a weekday if you prefer a less crowded experience.

There are two main ski-lift stations, which provide access to slopes suitable for all levels of ability. **Jonction**, directly above Ouyoun es-Simaan, is the largest with eight lifts (one baby slope, three medium-ability slopes and four advanced slopes). Further up the road is **Wardeh**, where there are a further seven ski lifts leading to three baby slopes, two medium-ability slopes and two advanced slopes.

Visitors staying at the Mzaar Intercontinental Hotel have access to a third ski-lift centre, which operates from the hotel grounds. Known as the **Refuge**, this centre has two ski lifts both accessing medium level-slopes.

The 'Mzaar' chairlift at Jonction reaches the highest point of the resort (2465 m) from where there are stunning views out over the Bekaa Valley to the east, Mount Hermon to the south, Laqlouq and The Cedars to the north and the Mediterranean to the west. The resort has two snow machines that can be used on even the steepest slopes. Snowploughs are on hand to keep the main road up to the resort open throughout the season. Various skiing competitions are held from February to March and there is occasionally floodlit night skiing on the 'Refuge' slopes.

Skiing lessons can be arranged and ski equipment is available for hire at both Jonction and Wardeh as well as through the hotels in Faraya and Ouyoun es-Simaan. There are also a number of ski-hire shops in Faraya and on the main road between Aajaltoun and Faraya.

Faqra → *For listings, see pages 85-88.*

There's no village here as such, except for the artificial 'village' of the Faqra Ski Club, which is a private members-only ski field. The surrounding scenery here is beautiful, though it is fast disappearing under a sea of chalet complexes. At the moment massive cranes dominate the skyline along the road to Faqra Ski Club, busy with all the new construction work going on.

Even if you can't ski at Faqra club itself, the short trip here from Faraya is worthwhile to visit the Faqra temple ruins and to see the bizarre natural rock bridge.

Skiing at Faqra Club
① *Mon-Fri 0800-1530, Sat-Sun/public holidays 0800-1600, weekdays US$12, weekends US$20.*
This is a private ski club complete with its own mini-village of privately owned chalets and a luxury hotel. The resort has one chairlift, two ski lifts and a baby ski lift, giving access to some 200 ha of slopes that are suitable for all levels of ability. To ski here you must be invited as the guest of a club member, although it may be possible to arrange to ski as a visitor here during the week when it is much quieter. Ring the hotel in advance to enquire.

Rock bridge
En route between Faraya and Mzaar, if you turn right at the checkpoint and junction (5 km from Faraya), after 1.5 km you come to a signpost for 'Pont Naturel Kfardebian', off to the right of the road. A short track takes you down to a rock bridge over a stream, looking for all the world as if it has been carved by hand, although in fact it is a natural feature, eroded by the forces of nature out of the limestone rock.

Faqra temple ruins
① *Daily 0900-sunset, 2000 LBP (though often the site is left open and the guard not here).*
Continuing straight on, you arrive after 1.5 km at a crossroads and sign for 'Archeologic sites of Faqra'. Visible off to your right, up a short track, are the remains of a curious cube-shaped structure, heavily ruined though solidly built of huge stone blocks. This is known as the **Claudius tower** and a Greek inscription above the entrance states that it

was rebuilt by the Emperor Claudius in AD 43-44 and dedicated to the 'very great god' (almost certainly Adonis).

The cube base was once topped by a stepped pyramid that has now all but completely collapsed. Inside, steps lead up onto the roof. Given its unusual design and the style of the stone blocks used in its construction, it seems likely that the building is actually much older than its inscription suggests. To the right of the track leading up to the Claudius tower is the base of an altar, while to the left of the track is another smaller altar that's been restored, with 12 miniature columns arranged like a mini *portico* supporting the altar top.

Turning left at the crossroads, 500 m away at the bottom of this road, are the more substantial remains of two **temples**, both within fenced-off enclosures. The larger temple (to your right as you enter) was probably also dedicated to Adonis. It is set amidst limestone rocks that have been eroded into bizarre fluted shapes and look almost as if they have themselves been carved by hand. In front of the temple is a squat structure of huge stone blocks that probably served as an altar. The walls of the temple enclosure or *temenos* are still largely intact, while, inside, extensive restoration work has been carried out, including the use of dubious amounts of concrete in the reconstruction of the six columns that formed the *portico* of the *cella*.

The smaller temple (to your left as you enter) was originally dedicated to the Syrian goddess Atargatis and later became identified with Astarte, before being partially dismantled in the Byzantine era to build a church. The basic outline of the temple still stands, consisting of a rectangular building divided into a large antechamber followed by a smaller inner sanctum. Low niches line the walls of the latter, while on the ground there is a large circular stone basin with carved decorations on it. Adjacent to the temple, the ten standing columns that can still be seen formed the nave of the church; carved on one of the fallen stones in the compound is a Byzantine cross.

Laqlouq Ski Resort → *For listings, see pages 85-88.*

① *Mon-Fri 0800-1530, Sat-Sun 0800-1600, weekdays US$16, under 15-years US$13, weekends US$23, under 15-years US$20, weekdays half-day pass (after 1200) US$11, weekends half-day pass US$15. On weekends during the winter skiing season, it may be possible to find service taxis running to Laqlouq from Byblos or from Dora Junction in Beirut, but otherwise the only way to get here is by your own transport or a private taxi.*

The ski resort of Laqlouq doesn't really have a centre as such; the first part you come to consists of the **Lavalade Hotel** and several chalet developments. Some 2 km further on, the **Shangri La Hotel** is signposted off to the right of the road. This hotel complex is close to the foot of the slopes, and there are a number of private chalet complexes nearby.

Originally Laqlouq was one of the smallest ski resorts in Lebanon alongside Qanat Bakich, but following development of the resort in 1996-1997 there are now three chair-lifts, three ski lifts and three baby lifts. Most of the slopes are quite gentle (suitable for beginners to medium ability), although one technical alpine slope has been approved by the International Ski Federation as suitable for Giant Slalom events at international competition level. There are also excellent opportunities for cross-country skiing.

As always, weekends are the busiest (and most expensive times) to ski. The ski school includes French instructors and has a good reputation. Skiing equipment is available for hire from between US$5-12 from shops on the road approaching the ski station and there are rescue and medical facilities on hand.

Cedars of the Lord

Known locally as Al Arz al-Rab (The Cedars of the Lord), the Lebanese Cedar is the country's national symbol, and a source of great pride among the Lebanese. Once, much of the Lebanon mountain range was clad in rich cedar forests (conservative estimates suggest that these would have covered as much as 80,000 ha), but their exploitation goes back just about as far as recorded history.

According to legend, Gilgamesh, the third millennium BC king of Uruk in southern Mesopotamia, came to Lebanon to cut down cedars for his city. Inscriptions discovered at Mari in Syria relate how the Amorite king Yakhdun Lim did likewise in the second millennium BC, while the campaign history of Tiglath Pilser I, the late second millennium BC Assyrian king, tell a similar story. There are also numerous references in the Bible to the exploitation of Lebanon's cedar forests by the Phoenicians of Tyre, Sidon and Byblos, both for the building of ships and for export to Egypt and Israel. Most famously, the Bible recounts how King Solomon's temple in Jerusalem was built of cedar wood beams, and panelled throughout with cedar, "So give orders that cedars of Lebanon be cut for me... So Solomon built the temple and completed it... The inside of the temple was cedar, carved with gourds and open flowers. Everything was cedar; no stone was to be seen." (1 Kings 5; 6, 9, 1 Kings 6; 14, 18)

The exploitation continued more or less unabated through the Roman, Byzantine and Islamic periods, right up until the trees felled by the Ottomans for use as sleepers in the building of the Hejaz railway, and during the First World War as fuel on the trains. Today, despite attempts to regenerate the remaining stands of cedars through planting schemes, there is evidence to suggest that they are under serious stress from pollution, soil erosion and infection, and that their ability to survive naturally in such small numbers is debatable.

The Cedars (Al Arz) → *For listings, see pages 85-88.*

When the French established an army skiing school here in the 1930s, The Cedars became the first of Lebanon's ski resorts. Today it is the second most popular ski resort after Mzaar and although not as developed, its higher altitude (maximum 2800 m) means that the season generally runs for slightly longer (mid-November to late April). Just out of town is the famous cedar stand, known locally as *Al Arz al-Rab* (The Cedars of the Lord), from which the resort takes its name. This small stand of around 300 cedars is all that remains of the once extensive cedar forests that covered this landscape.

During the ski season, especially on weekends, The Cedars gets extremely busy. In summer this tiny village is a sleepy, near dormant, destination during the week, though weekends see the resort slightly busier with local hotels awakening to The Cedars action-adventure potential. Many now offer mountain bikes and ATVs for hire, and this is also one of the main locations in Lebanon where you can learn to paraglide during the summer.

Arriving in The Cedars

Getting there Except during the ski season, when you may find a service taxi heading up here from Bcharre, there is no public transport to The Cedars. A private taxi from Bcharre costs around 10,000 LBP.

If you're driving, there are two roads from Bcharre. Following the road up out of town, signposted 'The Cedars', you can either keep going straight along the new road or turn sharp right (signposted 'Qadisha Grotto') to go via the **L'Aiglion Hotel** and the grotto. Both roads join up at the top of the plateau and lead to the ski resort (8 km from Bcharre). Further up, beyond the ski resort, is the stand of cedars itself.

Skiing at The Cedars

ⓘ *Mon-Fri 0800-1530, Sat-Sun 0800-1600, weekdays US$23, under 16-years US$20, weekends US$30, under 16-years US$20, weekdays half-day pass (after 1200) US$17, weekends half-day pass (after 1200) US$23.*

The excellent slopes and high quality of the snow have given The Cedars something of a reputation as a resort for 'serious' skiers. However, this is also a good all-round destination for skiers and snowboarders of all levels, with excellent cross-country skiing available here and a variety of gentle slopes for complete beginners to practise on.

As well as the main **Pic de Dames** chairlift, which reaches 2800 m, there are three ski lifts and four baby lifts. A gondola is also being constructed at the slopes which, when finished, will be able to transport skiers and visitors from the ski station up to the highest accessible summit at 2870 m. Ski equipment is available for hire from a number of the hotels from around US$5-12 per day, while, as well as renting and selling ski equipment, the **Tony Arida Centre** has its own skiing school with professional instructors. There is a duty doctor at the resort during the season and Red Cross teams in attendance on weekends. The main road up to the resort (via Amioun, Hadath el-Jobbe and Bcharre) is kept open throughout the season.

The cedar trees

ⓘ *Daily summer 0900-1800, winter 0900-1600, by donation (5000 LBP per person is appropriate).*

Today all that remains of the once extensive forests that gave the area its name is a small, somewhat forlorn stand of around 300 cedars in a landscape otherwise practically bereft of any trees. Although at first sight something of a disappointment, this stand nevertheless contains some of the oldest and largest cedar trees in Lebanon, rising to a height of 35 m and estimated to be between 1000-1500 (or by some accounts up to 2000) years old.

The steady depletion of Mount Lebanon's cedar forests has taken place over thousands of years, but it was only by the mid-19th century it began to dawn on the local people that they would soon disappear altogether. The Maronite Patriarchs of Bcharre placed them under their personal protection, building a small chapel in the midst of the stand in 1843 and forbidding any further felling of the trees. In 1876 Queen Victoria financed the building of a protective wall around the cedars, important for keeping out grazing goats.

Today, the **Friends of the Cedars' Committee** at Bcharre has taken over responsibility for protecting them, repairing the enclosure wall and marking out a path through the trees. In addition, there are various projects in place to carry out further research into the trees and to plant new stands in the surrounding areas. There are numerous souvenir shops around the entrance to the enclosure selling all kinds of cedar wood trinkets (carved from naturally fallen timber only), as well as a number of cafés and snack places.

Mount Lebanon Skiing listings

For hotel and restaurant price codes and other relevant information, see pages 9-10.

🛏 Where to stay

Faraya village and Mzaar Resort *p80*
Most of the accommodation is in the form of chalets and apartments that are rented out for the whole of the skiing season and are often booked up as much as 1 year in advance. The hotel accommodation fills up quickly during the season, particularly on weekends. Price categories below are for the high season. Substantial discounts (often as much as 50%) are available in the low season (this is basically when there is no snow; ie from around late Apr/early May until Nov/Dec).

During winter telephone lines are invariably broken by storms, so most of the hotels make use of mobile phone numbers (code 03) as well as landlines.

$$$$ Mzaar InterContinental, Ouyoun es-Simaan, T09-340100, www.intercontinental. com. This low-rise resort is a tasteful blend of wood and traditional stone and boasts direct access to the slopes with its own ski lifts. Everything you could need is here – excellent restaurants, bar, pool, gym and a luxurious spa, plus tonnes of sports and activities on offer. The rooms are flooded with light and have balconies and come with all the usual mod cons, though the decor is unfortunately rather bland. Note that the slightly cheaper standard rooms are near identical to the deluxe rooms except that they are a little further from the core of the hotel. During low season there are generally good discounts to be found.
$$$ Merab, Ouyoun es-Simaan, T09-341341, www.merabhotel.com. The stylish rooms at this wonderfully friendly and family-run place are cosy and comfortable and there are larger (and more expensive) suites for families. All come with satellite TV and minibar and most have small balconies.

It's an excellent choice, with a good restaurant and a free morning shuttle to the slopes for guests. Recommended.
$$ Al Badre, main road, Faraya village, T03-749 999, www.albadrhotel.com. This curiously designed hotel has welcoming management who are happy to help. Families or friends can stay in a 2-bedroom chalet (complete with kitchenette, satellite TV and log fire) where loads of dark wood has been used to create an alpine-cabin feel. The only complaint is that they're a little pokey for 4 people. There are cheaper split-level studio-style rooms upstairs (satellite TV, balcony) and even the smaller (and cheaper) ones still come with kitchenette, making them perfect for those trying to cut down costs by eating in. Recommended.
$$ Tamerland, main road between Faraya and Ouyoun es-Simaan, T09-321268, www.tamerlandhotel.com. This lovely old building is set back from the road and surrounded with trees. The decently sized rooms here are a homely and quiet choice and come with private balcony. There are also bigger (2 bedroom) apartments with kitchenettes that are excellent for families. Breakfast included, Wi-Fi.
$ Coin Vert, main road, Faraya, T09-321556, T03-724611. Stuck in a 1970s time warp, when pine-wood clad interiors were the height of hotel chic, Coin Vert is Faraya's top budget choice. The rooms are nothing to write home about; small and a tad dreary with threadbare carpets and miniscule bathrooms, but they're clean and bright, with most possessing tiny balconies. Staff and management are helpful and smiley. Ask to see a few rooms before deciding as some are better than others. Recommended.

Faqra *p81*
$$$$ Auberge de Faqra, Faqra Ski Club, T09-300600, www.faqraclub.com. This large complex right by Faqra's slopes boasts a heated pool, restaurants, bar,

spa/health club and access to all sorts of sport and activity facilities. The rooms are comfortable, though overpriced. Breakfast included.

$$$$-$$$ Terrebrune, on road to Faqra Club, T09-300060, T03-030301, www. terrebrunehotel.com. This stylish and slick hotel is the height of modern luxury with its mix of traditional stone walls, neutral decor and snazzy low-lighting. The quiet rooms here (a/c, satellite TV, minibar, Wi-Fi) are large and swish with spacious bathrooms and either a terrace or balcony. There are lots of little extras to make your stay comfortable, with a good range of bath products in the bathroom and tea/coffee-making facilities in all rooms. The hotel is open all year and can arrange ATV and mountain-biking trips in summer. The outdoor pool has incredible views.

The Cedars (Al Arz) *p83*

Price categories are for the winter skiing season; outside of this period expect substantial discounts. Note that many of the hotels offer apartments that come with kitchenettes and some can sleep up to 10 or so people, making them excellent value if you are travelling with a group of friends. Others offer the option of ski packages that include full/half board as well, which can work out cheaper than just booking the room. All hotels below have heating in the rooms.

$$$$ L'Auberge des Cedres, take the right-hand turn after the Alpine Hotel and follow the signposts, T06-678888, T03-566953, www.smresorts.net. Away from the main road, this resort looks for all the world like it has been transported directly from the Swiss Alps with its beautiful wood facade all covered in vines. Inside, lovely old *kilims* and carpets cover the floors and add a local feel to the otherwise traditional county-lodge decoration with lots of dark wood and quaint old-worldy touches to make the rooms feel cosy. During summer months guests can also stay in their luxury

tents. The staff here are ultra friendly and can help arrange all sorts of activities.

$$$$-$$$ Toni Arida Centre, main road, T06-678195, T03-321998, habibarida@ yahoo.com. This is a 1-stop shop for skiers and snowboarders, owned and run by Toni Arida, Lebanon's first qualified ski instructor and quite a character. With ski shop and ski rental, a ski school and access to their own baby-lift/beginners' slopes, as well as a restaurant and nightclub, the centre has all bases covered. There's a selection of cosy apartments that all come with lounge (satellite TV, open fire), kitchenette and some severely dated furnishings. The larger (and more expensive) ones can sleep up to 8. Good value for groups, though rather overpriced for couples. Good discounts are available out of ski season.

$$$ Le Cedrus, main road, T06-678777, www.cedrushotel.com. Unfortunately the plush interior of the reception doesn't quite follow through to the rooms which, though large and comfortable (satellite TV), could do with the bathrooms being updated. Management are friendly and helpful, there's free Wi-Fi and the excellent Le Pichot restaurant is below. Breakfast included.

$$$-$$ Alpine, main road, T03-213102, elie2@hotmail.com. This hotel has a large homely lounge downstairs with a roomy bar and games room as well as a lovely outdoor terrace. Upstairs the selection of large, bright and comfortable rooms all have spacious bathrooms and small balconies. The more expensive ones come with magnificent views.

$ Auberge Ecoclub Bcharre, main road, T06-678999. On the road between Bcharre and The Cedars, the Auberge has cheap and cheerful dorm beds on offer as well as a couple of private rooms which make it a nice option if you have your own transport. There's a neat and tidy lounge to hang out in and the communal bathrooms are kept spick-and-span.

❼ Restaurants

Faraya village and Mzaar Resort *p80*
All the hotels have restaurants; most of them offer inclusive full- or half-board deals, so there's not that much in the way of independent restaurants.

If you're after a snack or a cheap meal there are a few simple places on the main road in Faraya village. 2 of the better ones are **Snack Bafaraya**, on the roundabout and **Quick Snack**, on the main road near the Coin Vert Hotel. If you feel like something different, the café inside **B Zone Internet**, opposite the Coin Vert Hotel, dishes up decent crêpes. Both the **supermarket** and **fruit and vegetable market** are on Faraya village's main road.

$$$ Le Refuge, Mzaar InterContinental Hotel, Ouyoun es-Simaan. Top dining with an alpine twist. If you feel like going retro, the fondue here is popular and there are 6 delicious choices. The perfect end to a day on the slopes. Inside the hotel there's also a couple of other options: **La Tavola** (Italian) and **Les Airelles** (classic French cuisine).

$$$ Pancho Vino, main road, near Franzabank, Faraya village. This upmarket restaurant has a mix of dishes that span a range of different international cuisines, with steaks, pizza and various Mexican specialities all appearing on the menu. Portions are decent though it can be pricey.

$$ Chez Mansour, in front of the Merab Hotel, Ouyoun es-Simaan. A great little place under the same friendly management as the Merab Hotel. Cosy and welcoming, this is a top choice if you want hearty and no-nonsense food at good value prices close to the slopes. Recommended.

$$ Coin Vert, Coin Vert Hotel, main road, Faraya village. Unpretentious dining and a decent budget option. There's a range of Lebanese and European dishes on offer, all at reasonable prices, in this simple and homely restaurant.

$$ Jisr al-Kmar, main road, near the roundabout, Faraya village. An excellent

and reasonably priced restaurant that serves up good Lebanese staples (all your usual grills and meze) year-round with an outdoor terrace for lazy dining in the sun during summer months and cosy interior dining hall for when it's snowing outside.

Faqra *p81*
Inside the actual Faqra Ski Club there are various options, including the restaurants inside the Auberge de Faqra Hotel.

$$$ Chez Michel, off the main road just below the turning for Faqra Ski Club, T09-341021, T03-694462. This smart and stylish restaurant/bar attracts a pretty exclusive crowd, so dress to impress if you want to eat here. Open throughout the year, Chez Michel serves high-quality Lebanese cuisine. During the ski season it's a top party venue with live music or DJs on weekend nights.

The Cedars (Al Arz) *p83*
As well as the hotel restaurants, there are several snack bars and restaurants at the entry to the cedar forest itself, open all year round. There are also a few places near the foot of the slopes, although most of them are only open during the skiing season.

$$$ Le Pichot, main road. The top restaurant here, with a menu that leans towards Italian but also covers a range of Lebanese and other international dishes. Mains average about 20,000 LBP, but if you stick to the meze or the range of pizzas and pastas (13,000-18,000 LBP), meals are considerably cheaper. The signature Le Pichot pizza (mozzarella, rocca, parmesan and ham) is particularly delicious.

$$ La Tombe La Neige, main road. A narrow little bar/restaurant right in the centre of town with a French-inspired menu. The nachos are tasty and there's a decent selection of soups and salads.

$$ Mon Refuge, Mon Refuge Hotel, main road. This is a cosy restaurant serving up hearty home cooking at decent prices. Pizzas, pasta and burgers and a great selection of grills.

⚐ Bars and clubs

Faraya village and Mzaar Resort *p80*
Après-ski activity mostly revolves around
Ouyoun es-Simaan, near the slopes. The
bar in the Mzaar Intercontinental Hotel is a
popular place to hang out and is open 24/7.
Down in Faraya village the less pretentious
Kayak Club is a great option for a drink.

⚐ Directory

Faraya village and Mzaar Resort *p80*
Medical services Services on the slopes
during the ski season include an ambulance
and qualified mountain rescue team,
with an additional doctor and Red Cross
team on weekends and holidays. There's a
pharmacy, main road, Faraya village.

Chouf Mountains

To the south of Beirut, running parallel to the coast, lie the Chouf Mountains. Less ruggedly wild than the Lebanon Mountains further north, the Chouf is home to large swaths of densely forested slopes speckled with red-roofed villages hugging the ridges, while intensely cultivated land dominates the valleys below.

Traditionally the Chouf Mountains were the centre of the silk industry, which brought great wealth to its leading families. It was here, at Deir el-Qamar, that the House of Maan, the Ottoman-appointed government of the region, established their seat of government in the late 16th century. Although a small and sleepy mountain village now, Deir el-Qamar has been left with a wealth of well-preserved buildings from this period, which have been carefully restored.

In the late 17th century the Shihab family took over from the Maans and in the early 19th century Emir Bashir Shihab II moved the seat of power to Beiteddine and built what today is this region's most spectacular monument. Beiteddine Palace is a sumptuous example of the opulent lives of the Emirs; its huge scale, exquisitely detailed mosaic floors and rich furnishings are a reminder of a time when the Chouf was a centre of politics and governance, rather than the quiet mountain backwater of today.

Background → *For listings, see pages 96-97*

From the 11th century onwards the Chouf Mountains were the stronghold of the **Druze**. The 17th century saw the arrival of the **Jumblatt family** to the region, having been exiled here by the Ottomans due to their rising power in Northern Syria, and they were soon exerting political influence again, eventually becoming one of the most prominent Druze families in the Chouf. The 17th century also saw increasing numbers of Maronite Christians come to settle here at the invitation of the Druze emir, **Fakhr ud-Din II Maan**, who is considered by most Lebanese as the founding father of modern Lebanon, see box, page 90.

In 1788 **Emir Bashir Shihab II** secured the position of Ottoman-appointed governor of the Chouf region, helped by the support of the Jumblatt family despite the Sunni Emir's conversion to Christianity. Bashir took great care not to emphasize his own faith, striving instead to achieve unity among his subjects through even-handed and just rule. His palace at Beiteddine had no chapel, and engraved on the wood panelling of the hall in

Emir Fakhr ud-Din II Maan – Lebanon's first founder

In 1590 the Druze leader Fakhr ud-Din II Maan was appointed local governor of the Chouf Mountains by the Ottomans, following more than six decades in which the Ottomans had struggled to subdue repeated rebellions among the Druze, many of them instigated by the chieftains of the House of Maan. Although the Ottomans chose Fakhr ud-Din in the hope that he would prove to be loyal and subservient, he soon rose to be one of the most powerful local rulers in Lebanon's history, succeeding to be the first local governor to unite much of present-day Lebanon under his rule and leading many Lebanese history books to characterize him as the historical founder of the Lebanese state.

Initially he only controlled the Ottoman Sanjak (administrative district) of Sidon. Soon after, however, Beirut was added to this, and by 1621 he had extended his control to include the Maronite heartland of the Qadisha Valley, and the Sanjak of Tripoli.

In terms of developing and modernizing his kingdom, Fakhr ud-Din drew much of his inspiration from Europe. From 1613-1618 he was forced into exile in the Italian duchy of Tuscany after entering into a treaty with Ferdinand I, the Medici grand duke of Tuscany, which included a secret military article against the Ottomans. During his stay in Florence he picked up many ideas, and on his return set about expanding, strengthening and modernizing his kingdom with great zeal. New agricultural techniques were applied throughout the kingdom, with the development of the silk industry forming one of the mainstays of the economy (and also providing the impetus for the migration of Maronite Christian families into the Chouf Mountains, see page 173). Fakhr ud-Din was also responsible for carefully nurturing trading relations with Europe, and it was under his auspices that European trading missions in Lebanon, notably French and Tuscan, first became firmly established.

Ultimately, however, the Ottomans became uneasy at his growing power. In 1633 they ordered the pashas of Syria and Egypt to march against him, also sending a fleet of ships to attack the coastal towns. His son Ali led a brave resistance, but was eventually captured and beheaded, while Fakhr ud-Din was forced to flee from his capital at Deir el-Qamar, before being captured and taken to Constantinople. Two years later, on 13 April 1635, he was put to death, the Ottoman authorities fearing his influence even in exile.

which he held court was his motto, "The homage of a governor towards God is to observe justice, for an hour of justice is better than a thousand months of prayer." Bashir was noted for his enlightened rule, building roads and bridges and initiating irrigation schemes, as well as promoting health and education. However, despite his progressive ideas, Bashir was also a ruthless leader.

Once he had acquired the governorship of the Chouf he proceeded to consolidate his position, killing, blinding, imprisoning and exiling rival members of his own family and later turning against the Jumblatts as well. In 1825 he persuaded the Ottoman pasha of Acre to have the leader of the Jumblatts, Bashir Jumblatt, hanged.

In 1832 he allied himself with Ibrahim Pasha, the son of Mohammad Ali, who occupied Syria on his father's behalf. However, this state of affairs alarmed the European powers and in particular Britain, who feared that this upset to the balance of power in the region threatened her commercial interests. In 1840 Britain and Austria helped the Ottomans drive brahim Pasha from Syria. Emir Bashir Shihab II was captured and sent into exile. Just one year later Shihab rule collapsed and direct Ottoman rule was established, to be replaced soon after by a new arrangement which divided Mount Lebanon into two separately governed Maronite and Druze enclaves.

Since their arrival in the Chouf under Fakhr ud-Din II Maan's patronage, the Christian and Druze population had lived in comparative harmony, but as the Christian population of the region grew in number so did their call for a more equal share of power. In 1858, disgruntled Christians began to defiantly challenge the power of the Druze. In turn the Druze trampled the rebellion resulting in a large-scale massacre of Maronites which would lead to an exodus of Maronites from the region, a process which was repeated during the civil war of 1975-1990.

During the early years of Lebanese independence the Druze leader **Kamal Jumblatt** became a key caller for a secular parliament not based along sectarian lines. Having aligned himself with the opposition and the Palestinians at the start of the civil war, the villages of the Chouf became a battleground during the first year of war between the Christian militias and opposition forces. The bloodshed only came to a halt with the arrival of Syrian troops into the region, who had intervened on behalf of the Maronites. Kamal Jumblatt's assassination in 1977 (usually blamed on the Syrians) led to his son, Walid Jumblatt, stepping into his shoes as clan leader; a position he still holds today.

During the Chouf's occupation by the Israeli army in 1982-1984, Christian militias were brought in by the Israelis to dominate over the Druze. In the wake of the Israeli pullout in 1984, the Druze assailed the remaining Christians of the Chouf leaving hundreds dead. Most that survived chose to leave the region completely.

Since then there have been concerted attempts to restore the largely peaceful relations that existed between the Christians and Druze prior to the communal conflicts of the 19th and 20th centuries. In 2000, after a highly publicized meeting between Walid Jumblatt and the Maronite Patriarch, Jumblatt promised a safe and welcome return to any Christian who wished to come back to live in the Chouf. In some villages and towns Christians have indeed returned. On the whole though, with many ex-residents now having set up new lives for themselves elsewhere in the country or overseas, the number of Christians returning to the Chouf is only a trickle compared to what it was when they first began to arrive on the invitation of Fakhr ud-Din II Maan.

Deir el-Qamar → *For listings, see pages 96-97.*

Although small and peaceful Deir el-Qamar has a distinctly unhurried air these days, it has a grand history as the one-time capital of the local rulers of Mount Lebanon. Late in the 16th century Emir Fakhr ud-Din II Maan made Deir el-Qamar his capital (abandoning his former capital at Baakline due to water shortages), and it remained the capital for the local rulers until the late 18th century.

Bordering the main square is a small pocket of graceful and carefully preserved 17th-18th century buildings. Concerted efforts on the Department of Antiquities in the 1950s helped ensure that the buildings from this period were carefully preserved and that new ones wouldn't spoil the overall effect. The proliferation of refined stone houses topped by red roofs spread out over the hill give the entire village a rather elegant appeal. It's a nice place to wander around for an hour or so if you're on your way to Beiteddine.

The town's puzzling name (it translates as 'convent of the moon') comes from an interesting symbol unearthed in some of the excavations carried out here. The symbol (a rosette containing an inverted crescent overplayed with a cross) is seen as proof that this was once the site of an important Phoenician temple dedicated to the goddess Astarte.

Arriving in Deir el-Qamar

Getting there and away Unless you've been lucky enough to find a service taxi heading to Beiteddine from Cola Junction in Beirut, there is no regular public transport to or from Deirel-Qamar. The easiest way to get here is to hire a car or driver for the day. You could get the bus to Beiteddine and walk down to Deir el-Qamar from there, but this could still mean you get stuck as private taxis in Deir el-Qamar (which hang out around the main square) are few and far between.

Places in Deir el-Qamar

Around the main square The majority of the interesting buildings are grouped around the main square. **Fakhr ud-Din's mosque** was first built in 1493 and later restored by Fakhr

Deir el-Qamar

Where to stay 🛏
La Bastide **1**

Restaurants 🍴
Al-Midane **1**
Gardenia **2**
Marie Baz Café **3**
Moon Shine Snacks **4**
Serail el-Bek **5**

Sights ○
1 Younes Maan's Palace
2 Silk Khan & warehouse
3 Jesuit School
4 Terrace
5 Synagogue

6 Palace of the poet
   Nicolas el-Turq
7 Fakhr ud-Din's palace
   (Marie Baz museum)
8 Ahmed Chehab's Palace
9 Church of Saidet
   et-Tallé (Notre Dame
   de la Colline)
10 Salle de Colline
11 Plaque de Martyrs
12 Fountain
13 Youssef Chehab's serail
   (Palace de Justice)
14 Fakhr ud-Din Mosque
15 Old Souk

ud-Din II Maan. Small and simply designed, its octagonal minaret nevertheless adds a graceful touch to the square. Note the minaret's slight incline; caused by the earthquake in 1630. Immediately behind the mosque on a higher level is the **old cobbler's souk**, which still houses some small shops and cafés.

Behind this again, on the other side of the road that climbs up around the back of the square, is **Younes Maan's palace**, boasting a particularly elegant entrance doorway. Younes Maan was the brother of Fakhr ud-Din II Maan, and ruled from 1613 to 1618 while his brother was in exile in Italy. The building is unfortunately not open to the public.

The **silk khan and warehouse** of Fakhr ud-Din II Maan occupies much of the northeast side of the square. Dating from 1595, the scale of these buildings reflects the great wealth generated through the silk industry. At the level of the square are the halls that were used as servant's quarters and stables. Upstairs, meanwhile, was the main part of the silk khan and warehouse, now housing the **Centre Culturel et Linguistique Français**. You are free to wander around the cultural centre, which incorporates a school and library, although large groups should get prior consent to visit. Note the beautiful open-arched window overlooking the main square. The library occupies what was originally the warehouse, built in 1616 to store merchandise, etc. From the road that climbs up around the back of the square, a terrace on the right allows you to view two interesting buildings from the outside. The first was the **Jesuit school**, while the second was the **synagogue**, dating from the 17th century.

Returning to the main square, adjacent to the silk khan and warehouse is **Fakhr ud-Din's palace**. Fakhr ud-Din built this palace in 1620: his earlier palace had been burned down by the pasha of Tripoli while he was in exile in Italy and, according to legend, after defeating his adversary Fakhr ud-Din built his new palace with stones from the pasha's fortress at Akkar. The palace, owned by the Baz family who acquired it in 1925, now houses the **Marie Baz museum** ① *daily summer 0800-2200, winter 0900-1700, 12,000 LBP, children under 12 8000 LBP*. This consists of a huge assortment (more than 100) of waxworks of Lebanon's major historical and political figures (and some international figures who, in some way, have contributed to Lebanese history). It's a bizarre collection of who's who, but it may appeal to some and does allow you a look at the fine interior of the building. There is a small caféteria in front and a bar beside it.

Next door to the Marie Baz museum is **Ahmad Chehab's palace**, also owned by the Baz family, though this building is closed to the public (Ahmad Chehab was of the same Shihab family as Emir Bashir Shihab II, the names Chehab and Shihab being interchangeable). This palace was built in 1755 at the request of Ahmed Chehab's wife, who refused to live in her first house where two of her sons had died. In 1784 Ibrahim Pasha lived here while coordinating resistance to Ottoman rule.

To the south of the main square, on the opposite side of the road, is **Youssef Chehab's Serail**, or **Palais de Justice** ① *Mon-Fri 0900-1400, free*. Today this serves as the local town hall, but parts of it are open to the public. Note the two carved lions in circles above the doorway, representing symbols of justice. The entrance leads through into a large courtyard, decorated with beautifully carved stonework and a variety of different keystone arrangements in the arches above the windows and doors. The royal apartment occupies one side of the courtyard: there is a central dome in the ceiling and in one wall a large square bay window, complete with its beautiful original wood panelling, looking out across the valley towards Beiteddine. One doorway from the courtyard gives onto a steep flight of stairs leading up to the roof.

Churches quarter Reached via the small road that winds its way steeply down into the valley and then up again to provide a direct route across to Beiteddine is the **Church of Saidet et-Tallé** (literally 'Our Lady of the Hill' or 'Notre Dame de la Colline'), and beside it a **Maronite monastery**. Though in its present form the church dates mostly from the 16th century onwards, it is believed to have been built originally in AD 451, on the site of a temple dedicated to the goddess Astarte, before being destroyed by an earthquake in AD 859. The church is the focus of a major feast dedicated to the Virgin Mary, held each year on the first Sunday in August, attracting pilgrims from far and wide. In the large courtyard of the church is the **Plaque de Martyrs**, commemorating those who died in the massacres of 1860. On the south side of the church, carved above the original doorway, is a rosette containing a cross and an inverted crescent; the symbol from which Deir el-Qamar takes its name.

Off to the right of the road leading past the Church of Saidet el-Tallé there are a couple more churches down narrow cobbled streets, the 17th-century **Our Lady of the Rosary** and the 18th-century Greek-Catholic church of St Elie, which contains the tomb of Emir Bashir's favourite poet, Nicolas Turk.

Moussa Castle ① *On the main road to Beiteddine, 2 km east of Deir el-Qamar, daily 0800-1800, 10,000 LBP, www.moussacastle.com.lb.* Incredibly popular with regional tourists, the hilariously kitsch Moussa Castle is the handiwork of Mr Moussa, who as a lad was ridiculed and beaten by his school teacher for daring to dream of living in a castle. Having achieved success as a businessman, Moussa's wife encouraged him to follow his dream and he set about pouring much of his wealth into building the edifice you see today (turrets and all). He then opened the castle to the public as a museum. Each of the rooms here has been crammed full of a wide and eclectic collection of costumed mannequins portraying scenes from Lebanese history, religious tableaux and other montages.

Some of the mannequin scenes are absolutely hysterical – look out especially for the prehistoric, blond, Barbarella-style cavewomen, and the room downstairs that's given over to depicting Moussa as a young child being beaten by his schoolmaster for dreaming of his castle. Elsewhere there are also surprisingly excellent displays of antique swords and old guns that have been passed down through Moussa's family. The great man himself is often on hand at the entrance and is happy to tell you his personal story. It's complete tacky brilliance, and if you have a sense of humour it's definitely worth a stop.

Beiteddine → *For listings, see pages 96-97.*

The village of Beiteddine is the setting for the beautifully restored palace built by the **emir Bashir Shihab II** in the early 19th century. This is among the most impressive sights in Lebanon dating from this period. Its grand scale, elegant architecture and sumptuous interiors give some idea of the power and independence that Bashir achieved as the Ottoman-appointed governor of what was to become Mount Lebanon.

Arriving in Beiteddine
Getting there and away There's a minibus that leaves from near Cola Junction in Beirut, and travels up through the Chouf, passing Kfar Grotto before turning off the major Chouf road and then heading through the town of Baakline and passing very near to the town of Beiteddine itself before continuing on its way. If you take this bus you'll be dropped at the roundabout, about 1.5 km out of town. There's usually a taxi or two hanging about here, which will ferry you into the main square for 2000 LBP, or it's an easy walk into town. The palace is well signposted from the main square. Take the first left turn from the square and the entrance is a two-minute walk away down the road.

Alternatively, if you're in Deir el-Qamar, there is a minor road that also makes a pleasant walk to Beiteddine. Bear right at Youssef Chehab's Serail in Deir el-Qamar (coming in from the coast). The road descends steeply to the bottom of the valley and then climbs directly up to Beiteddine (3 km).

If you're driving from Deir el-Qamar, the main road through town continues east, past Moussa castle (2 km) before rounding the head of the valley, just after which a very sharp left turn (4 km) leads towards the Beirut–Damascus highway via Barouk and Ain Zhalta. The main road, meanwhile, continues on to Beiteddine (6 km from Deir el-Qamar).

Background
Beiteddine translates literally as 'House of Faith' and the palace was in fact built around a former Druze hermitage. Bashir employed the very best artisans and craftsmen from Damascus and Aleppo for its construction, as well as architects from Italy. According to some sources the palace took 30 years to complete. After Bashir was sent into exile in 1840,

t was used by the Ottomans as a government building. During the French Mandate period it served as a local administrative office before being declared a historic monument with restoration work starting in 1934.

After independence the palace was used as the summer residence of the president. During the civil war it suffered heavy damage, but after 1984, when the fighting in the Chouf had receded, the Druze leader Walid Jumblatt ordered restoration work to be carried out. Today the palace serves once again as the president's summer residence, so sections of it are closed to the public.

Beiteddine Palace
ⓘ *Summer Tue-Sun 0900-1800, winter 0900-1600, 10,000 LBP, students 2000 LBP. Guides are on hand at the entrance.*

Approaching the main entrance, note the lions above the entrance doorway, as on Youssef Chehab's Serail in Deir el-Qamar.

Leaving the entrance hall you find yourself in a huge courtyard, open on one side to give views out over the valley. This first outer section of the palace is known as the **Dar el-Baraniyyeh**. Along the entire length of the right-hand side of the courtyard is a long vaulted hallway supported by a double line of columns. Halfway along stairs give access to the upper floor (usually off-limits to visitors), consisting of an open terrace with a series of interconnected rooms behind. These two floors provided accommodation for guests, with sleeping quarters above and stables below. Offering hospitality to passers-by was a matter of honour, particularly among people of social standing. According to tradition, visitors could stay for up to three days without having to reveal their identity or their business.

Returning to the main courtyard, at the western end a double staircase leads up to an elaborately decorated doorway leading through to the middle section of the palace, known as the **Dar el-Wousta**. The vaulted entrance hallway leads through to a beautiful **courtyard** with a central fountain and graceful arcades around the sides. The arcades on the north and west sides are on the upper floor and reached by double stairs.

The southern side of the courtyard consists of an open raised terrace, once again

Beiteddine Palace

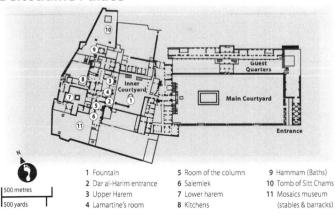

1 Fountain	5 Room of the column	9 Hammam (Baths)
2 Dar al-Harim entrance	6 Salemlek	10 Tomb of Sitt Chams
3 Upper Harem	7 Lower harem	11 Mosaics museum
4 Lamartine's room	8 Kitchens	(stables & barracks)

providing views out over the valley. The rooms around this courtyard were used as reception rooms, conference rooms and offices and are all very beautifully decorated with wood panelling, gold and silver leaf, marble, etc. One of the conference rooms is equipped with a small separate conferring room; inside, an arrangement of water flowing over marble served both as a cooling device and as a means of drowning out voices to allow privacy during delicate negotiations. The upper floor arcade on the west side of the courtyard (opposite you as you enter) boasts particularly beautifully decorated stonework. This is the **upper harem** of the Dar al-Harim; the room to the left is known as **Lamartine's room**, it was here that the poet stayed when he visited in 1833. Much of this area, together with the Dar al-Harim beyond it, is officially closed to the public, though exactly which rooms are closed depends on whether the president is in residence and/or holding audiences when you visit.

To the left of the double staircase leading to the upper harem is a monumental archway and behind it a richly decorated doorway providing access to the inner section of the palace, or **Dar al-Harim**. The doorway leads first into a waiting room, known as the **room of the column** due to the single column in the centre supporting the vaulted ceiling. To the south of this is the reception hall or **salemlek**, built on two levels with a beautiful mosaic floor and richly decorated marble walls. It was here that Bashir would hold court; on one of the walls is inscribed the motto that underpinned Bashir's philosophy of government.

To the west of the waiting room is the **lower harem** or private living quarters of Bashir and his family, consisting of a small courtyard with two iwans and rooms arranged around it. To the north of this are the kitchens, which in their heyday served up enough food to feed more than 500 people each day. To the north of the kitchens are the palace's **hammam** or baths (accessible also via a doorway from the courtyard of the Dar el-Wousta), consisting of a series of elaborately decorated rooms; the frigidarium (cold room), tepidarium (warm room) and caldarium (hot room). To the north of the baths is a shaded garden, in one corner of which is the **tomb of Sitt Chams**, the first wife of Bashir. The ashes of Bashir, brought back from Turkey in 1947, are also contained in the tomb.

Returning to the Dar el-Baraniyyeh (the outer section of the palace), to the left of the double staircase giving access to the Dar el-Wousta or middle section, steps lead down to a series of large vaulted halls that served as stables and barracks. These were large enough to accommodate 600 horses and their riders, as well as 500 foot-soldiers. Today the stables and barracks house a **mosaics museum** containing an impressive collection of mosaics gathered from various sites around Lebanon. The majority come from a fifth/sixth-century Byzantine church uncovered during the course of excavations at Jiyyeh (ancient Porphyrion), on the coast 30 km to the south of Beirut. Some of the mosaics have been incorporated into an area of garden adjacent to the stables/barracks.

Chouf Mountains listings

For hotel and restaurant price codes and other relevant information, pages 9-10.

🛏 Where to stay

Deir el-Qamar *p91, map p92*
$$ Hotel Libanais, T03-513766, www.hotelibanais.com. Hotel Libanais offers

a B&B experience. Reservations (at least 48 hrs' notice) are required.
$$ La Bastide, left-hand turn 1 km out of town, on the main road running to Beiteddine, T05-505320. This friendly, family-run place offers spotlessly clean and pleasantly furnished rooms, some of which have a kitchenette. Try to get a front-facing

room, which have balconies and impressive views across the valley to Beiteddine.

Beiteddine *p94*

$$$$ Mir Amin Palace, left-hand turn 1 km out of the centre of Beiteddine, heading south on the road to Jezzine, T05-501315, www.miraminpalace.com. Built by Emir Bashir Shihab II for his 3rd son, Emir Amin, this smaller but equally lavish version of Beiteddine Palace has been beautifully restored and offers panoramic views from its hilltop location. The 22 individually decorated rooms are tastefully elegant, luxuriously appointed (a/c, satellite TV, minibar), and scattered with antiques. If you visit out of season there are excellent discounts available. Restaurants, bar, swimming pool, breakfast included.

🍴 Restaurants

Deir el-Qamar *p91, map p92*
The **Marie Baz café** right in front of the Marie Baz museum is a nice place for a coffee. For a cheap and cheerful meal there are several simple snack places along the main road through the village, including **Moon Shine Snacks**, which serves up decent sandwiches just across from the main square.

$$ Al-Midane, just behind the mosque on the main square. A great little restaurant and café that's perfect for lunch after wandering around town. There are good salads and sandwiches (6000 14,000 LBP) for those who just want a light bite and more substantial mains (pasta, pizza and grills, 9000-20,000 LBP) for those after something more hearty.

$$ Gardenia, main road, on the right as you enter the village coming from the coast. This large restaurant offers typical Lebanese cuisine for around US$10-15 per head and has a shaded terrace to sit out on.

$$ Serail el-Bek, main road, next to the Serail. A very similar setup to Al-Midane across the road. This place serves some decent meze and its shady terrace is a good place to sit back with a drink on a hot day.

🎉 Festivals

Deir el-Qamar *p91, map p92*
Jul-Aug Deir el-Qamar Festival, www.deirelqamarfestival.org. This festival does a good job of promoting young talent and is an excellent opportunity to see up-and-coming local Lebanes performers.

Beiteddine *p94*
Jul-Aug Beiteddine Festival, www.beiteddine.org. The palace grounds provide a dramatic setting for a selection of concerts during the summer months.

🚌 Transport

Deir el-Qamar *p91, map p92*
There is, unfortunately, no regular public transport to or from Deir el-Qamar. You could take the bus to Beiteddine and walk down to Deir el-Qamar (there's a 3-km short cut you can take from right by the palace to Deir el-Qamar that takes you across the valley – ask any of the staff at the palace to show you the way). From Deir el-Qamar you would have to hire a taxi to take you back to Beirut.

Beiteddine *p94*
Minibuses heading to **Beirut's** Cola Junction bus station (1 hr, 2500 LBP) can be flagged down from the roundabout exit to Beiteddine. From the palace exit, walk up to the main square and then take the right turn exit signposted 'to Jezzine'. It's about a 10-min walk to the roundabout. Unfortunately the buses aren't particularly frequent. A few private taxis hang out in the Beiteddine main square if you get stuck.

Baalbek

Awesome in their sheer scale and mesmerizing in their richness of decoration, the ruins of Baalbek are, rightly, Lebanon's premier attraction. Known to the Greeks and Romans as Heliopolis (the 'City of the Sun'), these golden-stoned temples have been feted by travellers for centuries. Of the ruins, the eighth century Arab historian Mas'udi wrote "You will not find anything similar ... The height of the roofs, the dimensions of the stones, the length of the columns, the width of the doors, all this building complex is most wonderful." And it is. The massive dimensions are humbling. It is like walking through a city made for giants – a breath-taking example of ancient splendour that has endured the ravages of time.

Surrounding the ruins is the modern town of Baalbek. Due to the current situation across the border in Syria, Baalbek and much of the Bekaa Valley have been labelled no-go zones by many western government travel advisories. Check the situation carefully, and ask advice of local contacts in Beirut, before you decide to travel here. If you do decide to travel, please remember that Baalbek is a traditional town. Save your strappy tops for the coast and dress appropriately (shoulders and knees covered) to respect local customs.

Arriving in Baalbek → *For listings, see pages 104-105.*

Getting there

By public transport there are regular minibuses from Beirut to the Bekaa Valley town of Chtaura. Some minibuses from Beirut travel all the way to Baalbek but most finish in Chtaura or Zahle where you swap to another for the last leg of the journey. All minibuses arriving in Baalbek will drop you in the dusty car park beside the ruins, a short walk from the entry gate.

If you're driving, coming from Zahle the main route to Baalbek bears off to the right after 5 km (600 m beyond the turning for Furzol), bypassing the centre of Rayak, and then continuing northeast along a fast, straight road to arrive in Baalbek, 36 km from Zahle. If you are coming directly from Chtaura and the Beirut–Damascus highway, you can take the right-hand turning 4 km after passing Chtaura to bypass round Zahle.

Background

The holy city of the sun

Baalbek's origins go back to the **Phoenician** period. The earliest evidence of settlement dates back at least to the end of the third millennium BC, while during the first millennium BC a temple compound was established here, which became a centre for the worship of Baal. Of the history of Baalbek during the Phoenician period very little is known, but situated on the important north-south caravan route through the Bekaa Valley and surrounded by fertile agricultural land and on the watershed between the Litani and Orontes rivers and fed by water from its own spring, it clearly occupied a position of importance. The name Baalbek has variously been translated as 'Lord of the Land' ('Baal' translating as 'Lord' and 'Bek' as 'Land') or 'Lord of the Bekaa'.

Incorporated in the fourth century BC into the empire of Alexander the Great, it later became part of the **Seleucid** Empire. Equating Baal with their sun god Helios, the Greeks renamed the town Heliopolis. However, it was during the **Roman** era that Baalbek really came into its own. Having been made part of the Roman Empire by Pompey in 64 BC, the Emperor Augustus Caesar made it into a Roman colony, naming it Colonia Julia Augusta Heliopolis and settling a garrison of troops here.

Work on the temple of Jupiter itself started around 60 BC and was nearing completion towards the end of Nero's reign (AD 37-68). Under **Antoninus Pius** (AD 138-161), a grandiose series of enlargements were initiated, with work starting on the Great Court complex adjoining the temple of Jupiter to the east, and on the so called temple of Bacchus and temple of Venus. Finally, under **Septimus Severus** (AD 193-211) and **Caracalla** (AD 211-217), work on the Hexagonal Court and the Propylaea began, although some scholars attribute the Hexagonal Court to **Philip the Arab** (AD 244-249).

Baalbek

➡ Baalbek maps
1 Baalbek, page 99
2 Main temple complex, page 101

50 metres
50 yards

Where to stay
Jupiter 1
La Memoire 2
Palmyra 3
Pension Jammal 4
Pension Shouman 5

Restaurants 🍴
Al-Khayam 1
Cafés & Restaurants 2
Ras al-Ain Restaurants 3
Riviera 4
Sfiha Cafés 5
Tavern Cesar 6

Such was the scale of the undertaking that even with the advent of the Byzantine era, parts of the complex were still uncompleted. It has been estimated that the project employed the labour (and cost the lives) of more than 100,000 slaves over 10 generations. Artists and craftsmen from throughout the empire came to Baalbek to carry out the elaborate carved decorations and to produce the numerous statues which adorned the temples. Around 90% of the complex was built from locally quarried limestone, but the granite columns were imported from Egypt. They were shipped to Tripoli and then rolled along stone tracks around into the Bekaa Valley via the Homs Gap.

Baalbek after its heyday
Ultimately, Christianity triumphed over the pagan gods of the Romans. Under **Constantine the Great** (AD 324-337) pagan worship was suppressed, briefly reasserting itself during the reign of Julian the Apostate (AD 361-363), before being finally crushed by Theodosius I (AD 379-395), who ordered the destruction of the altars of the Great Court and had a basilica built there, using stones from the earlier Roman temples. Under **Justinian** (AD 527-565) a number of the massive granite columns from the temple of Jupiter were transported to Constantinople and used in the construction of the Hagia Sophia. In AD 634 it fell to the Muslim **Arabs** and subsequently became known once again by its ancient Semitic name. The main temple complex at Baalbek was later converted into a fortress, and although many of the stones from the temples were used in the defensive walls, these ultimately also helped preserve what was left.

Under Ottoman rule Baalbek fell into obscurity and, although visited in the 16th century, it was not until the visit of the English architects **Robert Wood** and **James Dawkins** in 1751 that the ruins were 'rediscovered'.

Baalbek in modern times
During the early 1980s several hundred **Iranian Revolutionary Guards** stationed themselves here and began preaching their radical brand of Islam, exhorting the Shiite population to embrace martyrdom as a means of overthrowing American and Israeli imperialism. Later it became the base for Islamic Jihad, Islamic Amal, Hezbollah and other radical Shiite groups, and in all likelihood it was here that the suicide bombers who wrought such terrible destruction on the American embassy in Beirut and later on the US and French military headquarters were trained. This is also where John McCarthy, Terry Waite, Terry Anderson and others were held for much of their time as hostages.

Baalbek is still a Hezbollah stronghold though it is more an administration centre for the organization rather than a military division. Unfortunately Hezbollah's involvement in the current Syrian conflict, and Baalbek's location close to the Syrian border, has ruled the Bekaa Valley a no-go zone in most government travel advisories. Be aware that you should check the most current travel advise before visiting here and, more importantly, seek safety information on journeying to Baalbek once on the ground in Lebanon.

Visiting Baalbek

Main temple complex
ⓘ *Daily 0830-sunset, 12,000 LBP, 7000 students. Guides are available at the entry gate, 30,000.*
Propylaea From the ticket office, walk round to the propylaea or **monumental entrance**. The stairs leading up to the propylaea were built during the course of German restoration work carried out in 1900-1904. The original staircase, which was more than 50 m wide,

was used in the Arab fortifications. The portico of the propylaea was supported by 12 granite columns, some of which have been re-erected by the Department of Antiquities in recent years.

On the bases of some of the columns are **Latin inscriptions**. The most clearly discernible one, on the third column base from the left, reads, 'For the safety and victories of our lord Caracalla'. The portico would have originally been covered by a roof of cedar wood and paved with mosaics.

Hexagonal court From the propylaea a doorway with a raised threshold leads through into the hexagonal court, the raised threshold serving to delineate the propylaea from the sacred enclosure beyond where sacrifices and religious dances, perhaps to the goddess Venus, were performed. The six-sided layout of this court is a reflection of the Eastern influences which guided the Roman architects. Thirty granite columns originally supported a covered arcade around the central hexagon, which was paved with mosaics and left open to the sky. The **central hexagon** is believed to have been covered over with a dome during the Byzantine era and converted into a church. The upper parts of the walls of the hexagonal court were added during the Arab period while the four rectangular exedrae around the court had arrow slits added.

Great court From the hexagonal court you pass through to the huge great court (or sacrificial court), where you begin to get a sense of the enormous scale of the temple complex. Around the north, east and south sides of this court were 12 semi-circular and rectangular *exedrae*, with numerous niches on two levels for statuary, and a covered arcade supported by 84 granite columns. Some of the columns of the arcade have now been re-erected, while scattered all around on the ground are numerous architectural fragments (some bearing inscriptions), allowing you to examine their richly carved decoration close up.

In the centre of the court are two large structures. The larger one to the east (of which only the lower parts are still standing) is believed to have been an **observational tower**, while the taller one immediately to the west of it appears to have been a **raised altar** where sacrifices were made.

➡ **Baalbek maps**
1 Baalbek, page 99
2 Main temple complex, page 101

2 Main temple complex

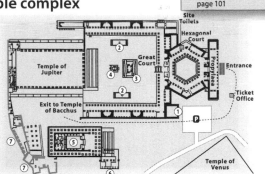

1 Museum entrance
2 Stone basins
3 Observation tower
4 Raised altar
5 Temple of Bacchus
5 Mameluke tower
7 Arab fortifications

The many faces of Baal

The god Baal was of Semitic origin, a sky god associated with the elements thunder, lightning, rain and the sun, and so essentially a fertility god, closely linked to the natural seasonal cycle. To the peoples of the richly productive Bekaa Valley, the importance of the cycle of the seasons for the success of their crops is easily appreciated.

Baal was synonymous with the Aramaean/Mesopotamian god Hadad, also a fertility god closely associated with lightning and thunder. References to Baal-Hadad have been found in Egyptian and Assyrian inscriptions, and also in the epic poems discovered at Ugarit (Ras Shamra) in Syria where mention is made of the rituals associated with Baal. According to the Ugaritic texts and later Roman writings, at Baalbek these involved licentious festivals where animal and perhaps even human sacrifices were made and sacred prostitution was practiced in a kind of human re-enactment of the cult of nature's fertility. Baal-Hadad's consort was Atargatis, goddess of the earth, in whom the fertility bestowed by Baal-Hadad found expression, while completing the trinity was a third god whose Phoenician identity remains uncertain.

Baal-Hadad was worshipped throughout ancient Syria, in numerous guises and with as many local interpretations of his attributes. The Greeks associated Baal-Hadad specifically with the sun and identified him with the sun god Helios, and with Zeus. The Romans meanwhile identified Baal-Hadad with Jupiter and his consort Atargatis with Venus, adding Mercury to complete the trinity.

Immediately to the east of the observation tower is a deep trench where archaeologists have excavated down to the original Phoenician foundations over which the great court was built. Also in the central area of the court, to the north and south of the altar and observation tower, are two large **stone basins** that most probably served as ablution pools where animals were ritually cleansed before being sacrificed. The basin on the north side is the more richly decorated of the two, with intricate relief carvings of cupids riding on sea creatures, medusae, tritons and nereids. Note how some of the carvings are unfinished.

Temple of Jupiter Ascending these stairs you arrive at the top of the huge raised podium on which the temple of Jupiter originally stood. Completely dismantled to provide stone for the Byzantine basilica and later Arab fortifications, today all that remains of the *cella* are the six massive Corinthian columns on the south side of the podium, which formed part of a *peristyle* of 54 columns surrounding the *cella*. The sheer scale of these six remaining columns, still standing undisturbed with their crowning *entablature*, having survived centuries of earthquakes, is truly awesome and one of the most enduring images of Baalbek.

Each column, consisting of three sections, is 2.5 m in diameter and rises to a height of 20 m, while the crowning *entablature* is nearly 5 m tall. Yet until you actually see them in all their enormity, it's impossible to comprehend their true size, and even then it's not until they are put into perspective by a human figure that this is really driven home. Descending to the open area between the temple of Jupiter and temple of Bacchus, you can examine a section of the *cornice* of the *entablature*, now lying on the ledge below the south side of the main podium, again giving an idea of the scale of the temple, and also the detail of the decoration which adorned it. The massive **carved lion's head** conceals a spout in its mouth through which rainwater would have been drained from the roof of the temple.

Temple of Bacchus Although dwarfed by the temple of Jupiter and as a result often referred to as the 'small temple', the separate temple of Bacchus is itself an enormous structure. More importantly, it is perhaps the most complete temple in the Middle East ever to survive from the Roman period, and apparently one of the most lavishly decorated. Monumental stairs ascend from the east to the massive entrance portal to the cella of the temple. The frame of the entrance portal is richly decorated with grapes, vines and other Bacchian motifs. The keystone, shown hanging down precariously in the drawings of David Roberts in the 1830s, has now been more securely pushed back in place and reinforced. On the underside of the keystone is a carving of a winged eagle carrying in its claws a *caduceus*, the snake entwined rod that was the symbol of the god Mercury, and in its beak a garland held up by two winged genii.

Inside the *cella*, the walls are decorated with engaged fluted columns and niches for statuary. At the far (west) end of the *cella*, stairs lead up to *adyton* (now vanished) where the image of the deity of the temple would have been housed. The peristyle surrounding the *cella* is still largely intact, its columns in places still supporting the massive stone slabs that covered the it. Elsewhere, these slabs lie propped up on the ground, the carved images of various gods today heavily weathered but still discernible. One of the columns of the peristyle leans precariously against the wall of the *cella*.

Museum ① *Entry included in ruins ticket.* Baalbek's museum occupies a vaulted tunnel that runs underneath the whole length of the eastern side of the Great Court. The museum contains some beautiful pieces of Roman statuary and architectural fragments, as well as numerous information boards detailing Baalbek's history, geography, strategic significance, method of construction, etc. If anything, there is too much information to absorb in one go, and no museum brochure to take away and read. A side room on the right towards the end of the tunnel contains a collection of photographs by the German photographer Hermann Burchardt illustrating everyday life of the Bekaa Valley at the end of the 19th century.

Temple of Venus

Opposite the entrance to the main temple complex, on the other side of the road, a fenced-in area encloses the remains of the temple of Venus (or round temple). At the time of writing the temple could only be observed from outside the enclosure, though in the future it may be opened to the public. Its tiny, delicate proportions are somewhat out of keeping with the massive scale of the temples of Jupiter and Bacchus.

The *cella* forms three-quarters of a circle, rather like a horseshoe, surrounded by a *peristyle* with five concave bays, each with a niche built into the outside walls of the *cella*. Originally a staircase led up to the podium on which the *cella* stands, its entrance preceded by a large rectangular *pronaos* topped by a triangular *pediment*.

Umayyad Mosque

Also opposite the main temple complex, to the northeast of the temple of Venus, is the Umayyad Mosque (or Great Mosque). Built by the Umayyads in the seventh to eighth century AD, the large square courtyard of the mosque has a pool and fountain in the centre, surrounded by four columns. To your right as you enter is a series of parallel rows of arched colonnades, the columns and capitals of which are clearly Roman in origin, taken from the nearby temple complex. In the northwest corner of the courtyard is the partially ruined minaret, its square tower terminating in an octagonal top.

Roman civic monuments
Opposite the Palmyra hotel is an area of excavations carried out in the 1960s. A stretch of colonnaded street lined with re-erected columns can be seen here, with a particularly striking column at one end topped by a fragment of richly decorated arch, appearing, with the help of a little reinforcement, to defy gravity. Across the road to the northeast of this is another area of semi-excavated ruins.

The Quarry
On the way into Baalbek (coming from Chtaura/Zahle), you pass the Quarry, signposted 'The Roman Quarry' off to the right. To get there from the centre of town, head southwest along Rue Abdel Halim Hajjar past the Palmyra hotel: it is signposted on the left immediately after the Coral petrol station.

Here you can see a massive slab of stone, known locally as Hajjar el-Qublah (literally 'Stone of the South') or Hajjar el-Hubla ('Stone of the Pregnant Woman' or 'Stone of the Mother Stone'). Although still attached at one end to the bed-rock, the greater part of the slab has been perfectly hewn into a rectangular block. Its dimensions are enormous (bigger even than the three 'trilithon' blocks in the west end of the podium of the temple of Jupiter), measuring 21.5 m by 4.8 m by 4.2 m and weighing well over 1000 tonnes. Presumably intended to form part of the terrace of this podium, according to one calculation it would have required 40,000 men to move it, although the builders evidently gave up and abandoned their over-ambitious undertaking. According to local superstition, when touched the stone has the power to make women fertile. There are several rock-cut tombs in the walls of the quarry. There is a souvenir stall beside the quarry, and a tea tent down in it. Considerable effort has gone into sprucing up the site in recent years: rubbish has been cleared, trees planted and the area attractively landscaped.

Baalbek listings

For hotel and restaurant price codes and other relevant information, see pages 9-10.

⊜ Where to stay

Baalbek *p98, map p99*
$$$ La Memoire, on the road behind the **Palmyra Hotel**, T08-373730, www. lamemoirehotel.com. The best hotel in Baalbek, La Memoire is set in a restored mansion that has been extensively modernized but still retains some of the character of the original building. Stone walls and wooden ceilings feature in the

rooms while the outside frontage has been completely renovated to create a snazzy, contemporary patio area. Rooms come with a/c and satellite TV and are all good-sized, bright and airy, but the ones downstairs are definitely the overall winners with their high ceilings and lovely old tiled floors. Restaurant, WiFi.
$$$ Palmyra, Rue Hajjar, T08-370011. Built in 1874 and boasting names such as Kaiser Wilhelm II, General Allenby and Charles de Gaulle in its visitors' book, the Palmyra is steeped in atmosphere and faded grandeur and 'faded' really is the correct word. Step

nside and you enter a world of crumbling glory where creaky staircases lead up to dimly lit narrow corridors hung with faded carpets and old oil paintings on walls of peeling paint. The rooms are smallish and are lacking in luxuries (some don't even have a fan) and come with bathrooms complete with rasping plumbing where hot water is only available in the mornings and evenings. It's the sort of place where you half expect a ghostly apparition to drift by. It's wonderfully charming in a stepping-back-in-history kind of way, but it won't be to everyone's taste and it's seriously overpriced for what you get. For those who want to say they stayed at the Palmyra but would prefer their room came with decent plumbing and a comfortable bed, the new extension has modern and comfortable (yet ornately furnished) rooms a short walk away. The extension also features a good restaurant that only opens when guests are in.

$ Jupiter, Rue Hajjar, T08-376715. Run by the fireball of energy that is Hani Awada, the Jupiter has a selection of large clean rooms with small bathrooms (fan, 24-hr hot water, some with satellite TV) catering for most budgets all set around an inner courtyard. The most expensive room has direct views over to the ruins while some of the cheaper rooms only have windows opening up onto the courtyard. It's a very welcoming place and Hani is a wealth of knowledge on the local area. Recommended.

$ Pension Jammal, Rue Hajjar, T08-370649. This friendly place has high ceilinged rooms (with fan) with attached narrow bathrooms. The comfy lounge area has a TV and management are extremely helpful. Solo travellers are well catered for with excellent value single rooms. Recommended.

Restaurants

Baalbek *p98, map p99*
Baalbek isn't exactly a gourmet paradise but it does have one delicious local

delicacy. *Sfiha* are square pastries topped with a succulent meat mixture which, if you've been to Turkey, you'll recognize basically as miniature meat *pide*. A really good place to try *sfiha* is at the tiny cafés surrounding the Hotel Jupiter on Rue Hajjar.

$$ Riviera, Blvd Ras al-Ain. The meze spread here is good value and the terrace is a great place to chill out for a leisurely lunch after a morning of traipsing around the ruins.

$ Al-Khayam, Rue Hajjar. This tiny, friendly sandwich shop is great for a quick bite, though you might want to steer clear of the 'brain sandwich'.

$ Tavern Cesar, beside Pension Shouman. This friendly, unpretentious joint dishes up a pretty good pizza as well as burgers and some good-value grills.

Festivals

Baalbek *p98, map p99*
Jul-Aug Baalbeck Festival, www.baalbeck. org.lb. Lebanon's premier annual event and the granddaddy of all festivals in the Middle East, the Baalbeck Festival runs a series of concerts set amid the awesome ruins of Baalbek across a 2-month period.

Transport

Baalbek *p98, map p99*
Minibuses heading to **Beirut** (2 hrs, 6000 LBP) via **Zahle** (30 mins, 2000 LBP) and **Chtaura** (45 mins, 2000 LBP) congregate on Rue Hajjar, opposite the Palmyra hotel. You can also usually pick them up in the parking lot near the ruins, where they drop people off arriving in town.

Directory

Baalbek *p98, map p99*
Medical services Ghasson Pharmacy, Rue Hajjar.

Contents

Footnotes

Glossary

A

ablaq alternating courses of contrasting stone, typical of Mamluk and Ottoman architecture (Arabic).

acanthus a conventionalized representation of a leaf, used especially to decorate Corinthian columns.

acropolis fortified part of upper city, usually containing a political, administrative, or religious complex.

adyton inner-sanctuary of the *cella* of a temple.

agora open meeting place or market.

amphora Greek or Roman vessel with a narrow neck and two handles.

apodyterium changing rooms of a Roman baths complex.

apse semi-circular niche; in a Byzantine basilica; this is always at the eastern end and contains the altar.

architrave lowest division of an *entablature* or decorated moulding round arch or window.

atrium courtyard of a Roman house or forecourt of a Byzantine church.

B

bab gate (Arabic).

barbican an outer defence, usually in the form of a tower, at the entrance to a castle.

barrel vault a vault in the shape of a half-cylinder.

basilica a Byzantine church of rectangular plan with a central *nave* flanked by two side aisles and usually with an *apse* at one end.

bastion strongpoint or fortified tower in fortifications.

beit house (Arabic).

bimaristan (*ormaristan*) hospital, medical school (Arabic).

burj tower (Arabic).

C

caldarium hot room in Roman baths complex.

capital crowning feature of a column or pier.

caravanserai see *khan* (Arabic).

cardo maximus main street of a Roman city, usually running north–south and lined with colonnades.

castrum fortified Roman camp.

cavea semi-circular seating in auditorium of Roman theatre.

cella the inner sanctuary of a temple.

chancel raised area around altar in a church.

clerestory upper row of windows providing light to the nave of a church.

colonette small, slender *column*.

colonnade row of *columns* carrying *entablature* or arches.

column upright member, circular in plan and usually slightly tapering.

crenellations battlements.

cruciform cross-shaped.

cuneiform script consisting of wedge-shaped indentations, usually made into a clay tablet, first developed by the Sumerians.

cupola dome.

D

decumanus major east–west cross-street in Roman city, intersecting with the *cardo maximus*.

deir monastery (Arabic).

diwan see *iwan*.

donjon (or keep) main fortified tower and last refuge of a castle.

E

entablature horizontal stone element in Greek/Roman architecture connecting a series of columns, usually decorated with a cornice, frieze and architrave.

exedra a recess in a wall or line of columns, usually semi-circular and traditionally lined with benches.

E

forum open meeting place or market.
fosse ditch or trench outside fortifications.
frieze central section of *entablature* in classical architecture, or more generally any carved relief.
frigidarium cold room in Roman baths complex.

G

glacis smooth sloping surface forming defensive fortification wall.
groin vault two intersecting *barrel vaults* forming ceiling over square chamber, also called a cross vault.

H

hammam bath house (Arabic).
haremlek private/family quarters of an Ottoman house (Arabic).
hypogeum underground burial chamber.

I

iconostasis screen decorated with icons separating the *nave* and *chancel* of a Byzantine or Orthodox-rite church.
iwan (or *diwan/liwan*) open reception area off courtyard with high-arched opening (Arabic).

J

jebel (or *jabal*) hill, mountain (Arabic).

K

kalybe open-fronted shrine with niches for statuary.
khan hostel and warehouse for caravans and traders consisting of walled compound with accommodation, stables/storage arranged around a central courtyard (Arabic).
kufic early angular form of Arabic script.

L

lintel horizontal beam above doorway supporting surmounting masonry.
loculus (plural *loculi*) shelf-like niche in wall of burial chamber for sarcophagus/corpse.

M

madrassa Islamic religious school (Arabic).
Mar Saint (Arabic).
masjid mosque (Arabic).
medina old city (Arabic).
mihrab niche, usually semi-circular and vaulted with a semi-dome, indicating direction of prayer (towards Mecca) (Arabic).
minaret tower of mosque.
minbar pulpit in mosque for preaching, to right of *mihrab*.
muezzin man who recites the call to prayer (Arabic).

N

narthex entrance hall to *nave* of church.
nave the central rectangular hall of basilica/church, usually lined with colonnades to separate it from the side-aisles.
necropolis ancient burial ground.
nymphaeum Roman monumental structure surrounding a fountain (dedicated to nymphs), usually with niches for statue.

O

odeon small theatre or concert hall.

P

pediment triangular, gabled end to a classical building.
peristyle colonnaded corridor running around the edges of a courtyard.
pilaster engaged pier or column projecting slightly from wall.
portico colonnaded porch over outer section of doorway.
praetorium Roman governor's residence or barracks.
propylaeum monumental entrance to a temple.

Q

qadi Muslim judge (Arabic).
qala'at castle, fortress (Arabic).
qibla marking direction of prayer, indicated in a mosque by the *mihrab* (Arabic).
qubba dome (Arabic).

R
revetment facing or retaining wall in fortification.

S
sacristy small room in a church for storing sacred vestments, vessels, etc.

salemlek area of Ottoman house for receiving guests.

sanjak subdivision of an Ottoman *vilayet*.

scaenae frons decorated stone façade behind the stage area of Roman theatre.

serai (or *seraya*) palace (Arabic).

souq market (Arabic).

stela (plural *stelae*) narrow upright slab of stone, usually inscribed.

T
tell artificial mound.

temenos sacred walled temple enclosure surrounding *cella*.

tepidarium warm room of a Roman baths complex.

tessera (plural *tesserae*) small square pieces of stone used to form mosaic.

tetrapylon arrangement of columns (usually four groups of four) marking major street intersections in Roman city.

transept transverse section between nave and apse of church, giving a cruciform (cross) shape instead of basic rectangular shape.

triclinium dining room of Roman house.

tympanum the space enclosed in a *pediment*, or between a lintel and the arch above.

V
vilayet Ottoman administrative province.

vomitorium entrance/exit to the seating area, or *cavea*, of a Roman theatre.

W
wadi valley or watercourse with seasonal stream (Arabic).

Index